GW01019046

THE BRITISH ARMY IN FRANCE AFTER DUNKIRK

THE BRITISH ARMY IN FRANCE AFTER DUNKIRK

PATRICK TAKLE

Pen & Sword
MILITARY

First published in Great Britain in 2009 by
Pen & Sword Military
An imprint of
Pen & Sword Books Ltd
47 Church Street
Barnsley
South Yorkshire
S70 2AS

Copyright © Patrick Takle, 2009

ISBN: 978 1 84415 852 2

The right of Patrick Takle to be identified as Author of this work has been
asserted by him in accordance with the Copyright, Designs and Patents Act
1988.aNo part of this book may be reproduced or transmitted in any form or
by any means, electronic or mechanical including photocopying, recording or
by any information storage and retrieval system, without permission from the
Publisher in writing.
Printed and bound in England
By Biddles UK

Pen & Sword Books Ltd incorporates the Imprints of Pen & Sword Aviation,
Pen & Sword Family History, Pen & Sword Maritime, Pen & Sword Military,
Wharncliffe Local History, Pen & Sword Select, Pen & Sword Military
Classics, Leo Cooper, Remember When, Seaforth Publishing and Frontline
Publishing

For a complete list of Pen & Sword titles please contact
PEN & SWORD BOOKS LIMITED
47 Church Street, Barnsley, South Yorkshire, S70 2AS, England
E-mail: enquiries@pen-and-sword.co.uk
Website: www.pen-and-sword.co.uk

Contents

Maps

Acknowledgements

I wish to acknowledge my gratitude to the following for their help and permission to publish extracts, photographs or maps:

M. Jean Claude Claire, Mayor of Veules-les-Roses, for his support and help in obtaining photographs of the tragic events in Veules-les-Roses in June 1940 and for permission to use these photographs. I particularly want to thank Mme. Emmanuelle Thivillier for providing copies of the photographs and of documents from the archives of Veules-les-Roses. Special thanks are also due to M. Yvon Debuire of Néry who translated documents and provided invaluable help in transmitting documents and photographs.

The Royal United Services Institute and its librarian John Montgomery, who provided ready access to their splendid collection of books.

Mr Andrew Orgill, librarian of the Royal Military Academy Sandhurst Library, for assistance and providing access to the Academy's many rare regimental histories.

The Library and staff of the Imperial War Museum for access to the Rommel Diaries.

Captain Fleming Jensen of Aarhus, Denmark for his introduction to the Maginot Line.

Finally, warm thanks to the staff of Pen & Sword for their patient help in drawing this book together and particularly to my editor, Bobby Gainher, for his assistance and forbearance.

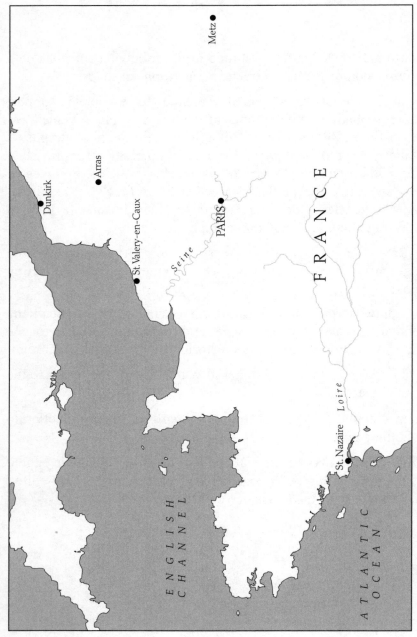

Map 1. General Map of North-West Europe.

Introduction

In May 1940 the poverty of the French and British approach to defeating Germany was exposed by the rapid advance of elements of the German Army through Holland, Belgium and northern France. The Allies had stood together for four years in the First World War and, after suffering huge casualties and some desperate exigencies, had eventually defeated the Germans in Northern France. Having declared war in 1939, the Allies had no better idea than to repeat the process by meeting and wearing down the German Army in the same area. In the inter-war years France had invested heavily in its Navy and Air Force and had also built a line of fortifications along part of its eastern border, which it considered practically impregnable, provided it was supported by 'interval troops' and mobile reserves. Only on the north-eastern border with Belgium was the frontier open, so the Allies dug in on that border and awaited the enemy's onslaught. The timidity and short-sightedness of this approach by the Allies failed to exploit their superiority in numbers of troops, tanks, ships and aircraft, and exposed them to rapid defeat by a far more determined and nimble enemy, who actually had better tactics and a plan for victory. At sea the Royal Navy had immediately demonstrated its courage and flexibility, but on land British ideas extended no further than defending the Empire and, as in 1914, standing on the left of the French line and following the French lead. As a result the rapid collapse of the French Army left the British hopelessly outnumbered and without any strategy other than continuing to do more of what had already failed.

Facing the collapse of his French ally, Churchill sought to do everything in his power to bolster their determination to continue the war against the apparently unstoppable onslaught of the Germans.

1

This account describes the reasons for the formation of the Second BEF, following on from the Allies' collapse in France and evacuation of the First BEF from Dunkirk. It follows the attempts, with Allied French units, to stem the tide of German advances in Normandy. It focuses on the dogged fighting retreat by the 51st Highland Division and 1st Armoured Division, as well as the eventual surrender of most of the 51st Highland Division to Major General Rommel at St Valery-en-Caux. It highlights the critical role played by General Alan Brooke in opposing Churchill's plans, and finally it covers the successful evacuation of Second BEF units from Cherbourg, St Malo, Brest and Nantes. These evacuations were so successful thanks to the efforts of the Royal Navy and partly because the focus of German attention was on the final defeat of French forces; but the inherent riskiness of evacuations, so far from Britain, was vividly illustrated by the fate of the *Lancastria*, whose loss in twenty minutes on 17 June 1940 took as many as 5,000 victims.

The miraculous success of the evacuation of the BEF from Dunkirk was achieved at a far higher cost than was clear at the time. Relief at getting a large part of the Army back to Britain had overshadowed consideration of the British dilemma of what it was to do with the many bases, aircraft and military units remaining in France after 3 June 1940, and how best to continue to support French resistance. The danger of throwing more units piecemeal into fighting the now overwhelming power of the Germans was vividly illustrated by the tragic loss of the 51st Highland Division at St Valery on 12 June 1940. Despite this dramatic lesson, Britain came very close to continuing to reinforce defeat by sending its last reserves to France in a forlorn hope to maintain a toehold of resistance, despite knowing that this policy had already failed in Norway.

In June 1940, 51st Highland Division was destroyed by the determination of General Rommel, who was not to be thwarted as the Germans had been two weeks earlier at Dunkirk, and he was determined to pursue the British closely to prevent another sea evacuation. Nevertheless, part of the Division did escape his clutches, and, together with some 160,000 British and Allied troops from Normandy and Brittany, reached Britain safely. Some battalions of the famous regiments which had been captured were re-raised and the Division was quickly reconstituted from parts of the 9th (Scottish) Division. Reformed and re-equipped, it travelled to the Middle East where it became the nemesis of Rommel as it ensured his defeat at El Alamein in 1942, and pursued him through North Africa and Sicily to his effective end back in Normandy in 1944. Here Rommel was severely injured about 60 miles from where the original 51st Highland Division had surrendered four years earlier. Rommel, one of the few legendary German battlefield leaders of the War, with the courage, reputation and integrity to rally the German defenders, was thereby effectively removed from the scene and prevented from continuing to resist the Allies or (as he undoubtedly wished) from agreeing peace terms. Hitler, recognizing the threat posed by Rommel, forced him to commit suicide in the aftermath of the July bomb plot. Even before his death, 51st Highland Division had broken through the German defences around Lisieux and had triumphantly liberated St Valery-en-Caux and Le Havre.

The following chapters describe the overwhelming forces and events faced by the Allies and the desperate efforts made by the pugnacious Prime Minister, Winston Churchill, to keep the French in the War. The resulting loss of a great deal more than the 51st Highland Division (and others) was only avoided by the determination of General Alan Brooke. In the end there was triumph for the Allies and the 51st Highland Division, but Britain at times came very close to disaster, and the fate of the encircled Scots at St Valery-en-Caux could have been shared by the whole British people.

CHAPTER 1

The Creation of the British Expeditionary Force in France

Following its Declaration of War on 3 September 1939, Britain began assembling an Expeditionary Force of four divisions in France (exactly the same as in 1914), with the aim of persuading the Germans to leave Poland, which had been the direct cause of the ultimatum to the Germans. Although the Royal Navy, under its newly appointed First Lord of the Admiralty, Winston Churchill, began warlike operations immediately, the rest of the British Government had no clear idea how the new war was to be won. The Allies seemed to be at pains not to antagonize the Germans by attacking them while they were still occupied in subduing Poland. So while German ships were attacked, care was taken not to bomb German cities with anything more dangerous than leaflets, while equipping and training for war proceeded slowly. Of course, it was difficult for the Allies actually to intervene militarily in Poland, so their preparations for a new war assumed it would proceed very much like the start of the First World War, with a German attack through Belgium followed by years of grim fighting in northern France.

In August 1914, the Germans had attacked France with seven large armies, of which three of them, on their right flank, had been used to invade neutral Belgium and then march in a wide arc towards Paris. These three armies comprised a force of some twenty-six infantry and five cavalry divisions, far stronger than the Allied forces which marched into Belgium to oppose them. The Allied left wing comprised the BEF of just four infantry and one cavalry division, and the French Fifth Army of ten infantry and two cavalry divisions. Outnumbered and outgunned the Allies had no alternative but to fall back in a fighting retreat to the River Marne. There a counter-attack from Paris on the German outer flank was mounted, and the hitherto retreating Allies were able to turn and drive the Germans back to the River Aisne, where the Germans dug in. This resulted in the stalemate of trench warfare for four years until the Allies eventually wore the Germans down and, in late 1918, were able to drive them out of France.

In 1939, Germany was still busy rebuilding its forces and was desperate not to become entangled once again in another long war of attrition fought on at least two fronts. Nevertheless, having absorbed the lands and industries of Austria and most of Czechoslovakia, the German Army was already much stronger in troops and equipment in 1939 than it had been even in 1938, when Chamberlain had reluctantly agreed to Hitler's demands at Munich. A non-aggression treaty with Russia took care of the immediate two-front problem, while Hitler sought radical solutions to achieve swift military decisions and avoid stalemate in the West. The campaign in the East against Poland, even though conducted with large bodies of marching infantry supported by horse-drawn artillery, also enabled the German Army to practise many of its new ideas, such as armoured (panzer) columns with their own artillery, engineers and integral motorized infantry speeding through and around the main enemy defences, closely supported by dive-bombers. The defeat of Poland was a major military success for Germany and its speedy conclusion by 27 September 1939 convinced many of the doubters that Hitler's reconstituted forces could also knock out France and Britain.

As in 1914, Britain and France were allied and expected a major German attack in the north of France. This expectation was based partly on the experience of centuries of history, as invaders chose to attack France through the Low Countries. It was also partly based on the French experience during the First World War, when they found that strongly defended old fortifications stood up well, even against modern artillery. As a result, during the 1930s, France had constructed a series of strong, interlinked, defensive fortifications along part of its eastern border from Switzerland to Longuyon at the edge of Luxembourg, called the Maginot Line. These fortifications were manned with some ten divisions, behind which were intended to be mobile reserves and an Army of Manoeuvre, which could be used to block any enemy breakthroughs. The French believed this combination of fixed forts and multiple defensive lines of infantry would, as in 1914, hold the Germans in this part of the frontier. the area of decision would thus be in the unfortified area on the left of the Maginot Line behind the border with Belgium.

By October 1939, the French had fully mobilized and the first British troops had started to arrive in France. To meet the anticipated German offensive, Britain had, by early 1940, increased its army in France to eight fighting infantry divisions, each of three brigades, organized into three corps. The army was well supported by a strong artillery component, which included field, anti-tank and anti-aircraft units. There was no armoured division (it was still in England and did not begin landing until May), but the BEF did have some ten armoured regiments. However, of these, there were only two heavy tank regiments in a single armoured brigade, and most of the formerly horsed cavalry and yeomanry regiments had been converted into lightly armoured reconnaissance units attached to infantry formations. The single armoured brigade was equipped with heavily armoured Matilda infantry tanks, but even these were mostly Mark I (armed with just machine guns) as there were only limited numbers of the Mark II, which mounted a 2-pounder gun. There were also two strong Royal Air Force contingents based in France: the Advanced Air Striking Force (AASF) consisted mainly of bombers designed to attack targets in Germany; and the Air Component which was a mixed force of fighters and bombers designed to support the BEF directly. Moreover, the British had also established a series of bases in northern France to support a far larger army, which was being equipped and trained for a rerun of the attrition of the First World War.

The French had mobilized over one hundred divisions, but the British, with a similar population, had, by April 1940, only managed to send ten fighting divisions to France (including two recently arrived divisions – the two-brigade 5th Division and the 51st Highland Division). A major problem for the British was a lack of trained and equipped artillery regiments to support infantry formations. This laggardly British effort aroused considerable French criticism as a result of which, in the early spring, partly to convince the French of the seriousness of British intentions, Britain sent over three more infantry divisions (the 12th, 23rd and 46th). These recently embodied territorial divisions came with no integral artillery or armour and were supported only by some Royal Engineer squadrons intended to assist construction activities. They comprised a total of some 18,000 very lightly armed infantry, who were grossly under-trained, having been used mainly for guard duties since their mobilization. Their role was to make up numbers, act as labour on the British Lines of Communication and continue the construction of the railway yards, bases and depots for the expanding BEF.

Once again, as in 1914, the Belgians attempted to avoid antagonizing the Germans by not deviating from their policy of optimistic neutrality. They therefore refused to co-operate with Britain and France in the defence of Belgium, despite the growing evidence of a likely German attack. As a result the four large French armies (the Second, Ninth, First and Seventh) and a relatively strong BEF, which were positioned north of the Maginot Line, remained in France, lining the border with Belgium. The two Allies then spent the winter digging in and preparing a strong but static defence line to meet an expected German attack through Belgium. Despite these extensive defensive preparations, the Allies had also perversely prepared a plan to vacate these defences and move almost the whole of this strong left wing forward to the River Dyle (covering and running to the east of Brussels) in the event of a German attack on Belgium. This Plan 'D' would involve pivoting on the French Ninth Army along the River Meuse, while the BEF and the French Seventh and First Armies swung forward to take up unprepared positions defending the line of the Rivers Dyle and Meuse within Belgium. The Belgian Army was expected to be able to delay the Germans on its strong border fortifications for many days while the Allies would help to defend Brussels.

This Allied force of some thirty-three divisions, under the overall direction of General Georges, comprised the cream of the Allied armies and could reasonably hope to support the twenty divisions of the Belgian Army and the ten divisions of the Dutch Army in halting any German assault. Although most French units still relied on horse transport, the BEF and the French Seventh Army on the outer rim of the wheel were both fully motorized and were the fastest to advance. They were supported by strong, locally based British and French air forces, but lacked good anti-tank and anti-aircraft weapons and integral armoured units. The French Army did possess three armoured divisions, but they were still deploying and training and were to be kept well in rear of the infantry armies as they moved forward.

The Germans, for their part, also still saw no viable alternative to putting their main effort through Belgium. Once again they planned to attack Belgium and France (and this time Holland) with an overwhelming force of some seventy-three divisions. However, to avoid being dragged into a costly war of attrition on the Champagne plains of northern France, the Germans had developed two major refinements to the old Schlieffen Plan. Firstly, they did little to dissuade the Allies from vacating their well-prepared defensive positions and plunging their left wing deep into Belgium, where they would be poorly prepared to meet the advancing northern group of two German armies comprising twenty-eight divisions (of which just three were armoured) under General von Bock. Secondly, the Central Army Group of three armies comprising forty-five divisions (of which seven were armoured and three were motorized infantry) under General von Rundstedt, focussed the centre of its attack on the southern part of Belgium and Luxembourg, at the juncture between the French Ninth and Second Armies holding the River Meuse around Sedan. This attack aimed to use a concentration of fast-moving armoured formations to achieve enough momentum to pierce the French Army defence line on the River Meuse and get into its rear areas before the French could reorganize their defence. Significantly, the relatively weak Army Group C, under General von Leeb, was left with just two small armies to keep French attention on the Maginot Line fortifications and down to the Swiss Frontier.

As a result, early on the morning of 10 May, within hours of the news of the German invasions of Belgium and Holland, the Allies (particularly the motorized French Seventh Army and the BEF) were quickly able to leave their well-prepared defensive positions on the French border and drive forward beyond Brussels to meet the anticipated German attacks coming forward relatively slowly from the north and east of Belgium. Most German infantry formations were short of transport and still depended heavily upon marching infantry and horse-drawn artillery. Thus the attention of the Allies was focussed on the direct threat of the slow advance by von Bock's armies, while von Rundstedt's much larger formations, with their mechanized spearheads, were able to approach the weakly defended Ardennes area largely unnoticed.

CHAPTER 2

Operation Dynamo

The Evacuation of the
First BEF from Dunkirk

The first attack in the West came on 9 April 1940 when the Germans invaded Denmark and Norway. Possession of these countries gave the Germans access to airfields and ports from which the reborn German Navy could threaten Britain with submarines and surface ships from along the whole of the North Sea. Denmark shared a short border with Germany and, with no natural defences, was occupied in just one day. Norway was a much larger country with difficult communications so that, in spite of simultaneous landings at seven ports and airfields, it took the Germans almost three months to occupy the whole country. Norway, despite being completely surprised, gave a good account of itself and moreover was soon supported by contingents from Britain, France and Poland. However, the failure of these troops to stop the German invasion was clear evidence of the general unpreparedness of the Allies and their lack of viable anti-tank and anti-aircraft weapons and tactics. On the other hand, the growing capabilities and confidence of the German forces was well illustrated by the fact that both of these military operations were carried out without diverting any real effort from the attack on Holland, Belgium and France, which started on 10 May (before the occupation of Norway had even been completed).

More worryingly for Britain was the evidence of the German ability to plan the same kind of effective 'combined operations' that they would need if they were to invade Britain. Nevertheless, although the occupation of Norway was a military success for the Germans, it was achieved at high cost to the German Navy. In its life and death struggle with the Royal Navy, the German Navy could ill afford the loss of three capital ships (*Blücher, Königsberg* and *Karlsruhe*) plus significant damage to four others (*Admiral Hipper, Lützow, Scharnhorst* and *Gneisenau*), and notably the total loss of ten destroyers at Narvik. Until more could be built, the German Navy was left with just four destroyers. Most significantly the high cost of the Norwegian operation left the German Navy incapable of supporting an invasion of Britain for at least a year.

The attack on Holland, Belgium and France was mounted by two army groups, comprising seventy-three divisions from a mobilized German Army of about one hundred and thirty divisions. Army Group B under General von Bock attacked in the north against Holland and Belgium. Army Group A, under General von Rundstedt attacked further south against Luxembourg, Belgium and France. At the centre of the attack by Army Group A was Fourth Army, commanded by General von Kluge. Its powerful spearhead was three armoured corps, comprising seven armoured divisions supported by three motorized divisions. The aim of these three armoured corps was to achieve both strategic and tactical surprise by moving through and around the 'impassable' Ardennes Forest. The creator of the German armoured forces, General Heinz Guderian, commanded the largest corps with three armoured or panzer divisions (1st, 2nd and 10th) which were given the vital task of breaking through the French defences around Sedan. His XIX Corps was reinforced by the addition of the crack Grossdeutschland Regiment and was followed by the three motorized infantry divisions (1st, 13th and 29th) of XIV Corps commanded by General von Wietersheim. This wedge of six, fast-moving panzer and motorized divisions was an extremely powerful combination. It guaranteed that Guderian would be able to rely upon rapid follow-up of his panzer units by motorized infantry, thus allowing him to maintain the tempo of his advance. The motorized infantry could, in turn, be relieved by the slower marching infantry of conventional divisions, allowing them to be able to follow the panzer units closely.

Guderian was a proponent of operational mobility in both the offence and defence, and believed that 'only movement brings victory'. He had practised and developed the theory of armour, infantry, artillery and air force co-operation, so he took pains to make sure not only that he worked closely with General von Wietersheim, but also that he had very good direct communications with his Luftwaffe support, both for reconnaissance and dive-bombing. Advancing north of Guderian's Corps was Panzerkorps Reinhardt (XLI Corps) comprising two more armoured divisions (the 6th and 8th). This grouped under the unified command of General von Kleist some eighteen battalions of tanks (almost 1,000 medium battle tanks) supported by motorized infantry, artillery and engineers, which would surprise and then slice through enemy formations. General von Kleist had another important task: to control Guderian and ensure that this ardent exponent of tank warfare did not imperil the whole enterprise by advancing too impetuously. North of Panzergruppe Kleist was yet another panzer corps (the XVth, commanded by General Hoth), comprising the 5th and 7th Panzer Divisions. Although 7th Panzer Division was the weaker division having only one regiment of tanks (three battalions of largely Czech-built tanks), it was commanded by the thrusting Erwin Rommel, who constantly sought to lead the race west. Rommel, an ambitious officer, had hitched his star to Hitler's and, by cultivating leading Nazis, had achieved rapid promotion from Captain to Major General in just seven years.

Rommel was determined to make his reputation in this war and in February 1940 he requested and was promoted to command a panzer division, a personal favour granted by Hitler. Rommel was already a distinguished fighting officer although he had never commanded tanks before. During the First World War he had been wounded twice and awarded the Iron Cross, First and Second Class. Finally, in 1917, with just 100 men against some 7,000 Italians, he had captured Monte Matajur on the Italian Front, thereby earning the rare distinction of the Pour le Mérite medal. However the medal for this achievement was awarded to another officer in error and Rommel had to pursue the unpleasant protest procedure before it was finally awarded to him. Rommel was not a warm man who seemed to feel that others conspired against him and that only by a constant struggle

13

could he achieve his just deserts. There may have been something in this for despite his outstanding war record, he remained a captain for twelve years. It was only in 1933 that he was given command of the Goslar Jaegers (the same regiment in which Guderian had served before the First World War). Without doubt his personal efforts (which he and Goebbels were swift to publicize), and his propensity to take risks, had made a success of his part of the Meuse crossing at Dinant and the containment of the British offensive at Arras, as well as the capture of Lille, including half the French First Army (IV and V Corps). Accordingly, he was awarded the Knight's Cross on 27 May 1940, which served to identify him easily to his soldiers as he usually wore it around his neck over the Pour le Mérite Star. Already by 25 May his division had suffered so many losses that it was necessary to merge its three tank battalions into one. As we shall see later, he also pushed his division deep into Normandy where he captured large numbers of French and British troops including the 51st Highland Division.

While Erwin Rommel received much of the publicity for the Army's success (particularly in Germany), it was Heinz Guderian who was the key figure in ensuring German success in the attack on France. He was the inspiration and leading proponent of the development of armoured troops within the German Army and understood fully their organization, equipment and tactics. He particularly understood the importance of communications (including radios in vehicles) and of working closely with the Luftwaffe to ensure air support for the success of his fast-moving units, which could otherwise easily outrun their artillery support. He had already practised and perfected this new 'blitzkrieg' form of warfare in the Polish campaign, when his XIX Corps covered 200 miles in just ten days. In addition, he had personally assured Hitler and the General Staff that his armour could traverse the difficult approach march through the Ardennes country (even though he had not tested this theory). The use of this unexpected route wrong-footed the French Command, who repeatedly responded far too late to a succession of unexpected German initiatives and were left floundering. The Ardennes approach route was a critical element of the German battle plan (originally conceived by General Manstein) to direct an armoured thrust at the junction of the weakest French armies. However, Guderian had also made clear his intention to exploit his anticipated success and to head for the Channel coast as soon as he had broken through the French defences on the Meuse (which he confidently expected to do).

The massive armoured thrusts supported by screaming dive-bombers against relatively weak French divisions dislocated the French defences, and events moved far faster than the French High Command could cope with. German troops crossed the Belgian border on 10 May and most of the panzer divisions had closed up to the River Meuse by the 12th. After relays of heavy air attacks and bold use of ground by Guderian's troops, they forced a breach between the French 55th Infantry Division and its neighbour in the Ninth Army, the 102nd Fortress Division at Sedan. The other two panzer corps also broke through the Ninth Army defences on the River Meuse at Monthermé and Dinant. The piecemeal committal of the three French armoured divisions failed to staunch this flow of tanks, and by the morning of 15 May, Guderian had broken through the main French defence line and was heading west from the Meuse crossings. General Guderian rested his left flank on the River Aisne, which protected him from a southern attack, but did not allow his spearhead units to loiter waiting for the infantry to catch up. With his rate of advance much faster than even his own commanders could anticipate, he was ordered to stop on the 15th (which order he disobeyed), and when stopped and disciplined personally by General von Kleist on the 17th, he asked to be relieved of his command.

Guderian received backing from other senior commanders who appreciated his success and the argument was patched up, allowing Guderian to continue his 'reconnaissance in force'. By the evening of 20 May, 2nd Panzer Division had reached Abbeville, practically on the French coast. The armoured breakout, led by XIX Panzer Corps, broke the French Ninth Army and resulted in the rapid outflanking and encirclement of the other three northern Allied armies, including the BEF. These three armies had withstood German frontal attacks and, although not initially defeated,

Guderian's bold advance had cut them off from their supplies and the rest of the French Army, forcing them to retreat in great disorder. Within days Boulogne and Calais were attacked and by 24 May, six panzer divisions and supporting troops were approaching the western outskirts of the Dunkirk perimeter. In the meantime the twenty-eight divisions (mainly marching infantry) of Army Group B had advanced through Holland and Belgium and were closing up to Dunkirk from the east.

Fortunately for the British, it was at this point that the main business of reducing the Dunkirk enclave was handed to the Luftwaffe and, on 24 May, the panzer divisions were ordered not to cross the Aa Canal. There were many reasons for this controversial halt order, which appears to have been originated by von Rundstedt and was then reinforced by Hitler. The marshy terrain around Dunkirk was difficult for armour and certainly all the panzers, which had driven hard for almost three weeks, needed maintenance before they were launched against the remnants of the French Army. (For example, 7th Panzer Division was halted for two days' maintenance and recovery after the Arras battle before it was launched, substantially reinforced, on the 26th in the major battle for Lille.) Time was also needed for the slower infantry units to catch up with the panzers as they were needed to overcome a hardening defence. Moreover, it was only sensible, having given the Dunkirk target to the Luftwaffe, to ensure that the precious panzers were kept well clear of the bombing and strafing attacks. As it was, the serious Luftwaffe attacks did not begin until the evening of the 29th. In addition, both Hitler and von Rundstedt were feeling cautious after the British attack at Arras and were wary of tanks being swallowed up by fighting in built-up areas, as the 2nd Panzer Division had been in Boulogne.

Interestingly, Guderian laid the whole blame for the order to stop at the Aa Canal on Hitler. His account is clearly somewhat biased (he later fell out with Hitler and claimed not to have supported him) and he admitted that, despite the halt order, troops under his command continued to attack over the Aa towards Watten, Wormhoudt and Bergues on the 25th and 26th. However, they were not able to take

Wormhoudt and Bourbourgville until the 28th, and Gravelines the following day, which is hardly evidence of the success of Blitzkrieg tactics.

The respite in panzer attacks allowed the British to organize the perimeter defence of Dunkirk and strengthen a defence line using the 48th, 44th and 2nd Divisions to reinforce the temporary Canal Line defending units, which had moved into position between the 18th and the 20th. In addition, French Army units from First Army moved into the line alongside the British and eventually continued the defence as the British withdrew. This strengthened defence line established on 24 and 25 May was vital as it was able to protect the main bodies of the BEF troops marching north. It also allowed the BEF to commence the evacuation of base personnel before commencing Operation Dynamo.

Fortunately, by 19 May, the British had begun already to make plans for evacuating part of the BEF using the Royal Navy. Small boats were assembled and it was initially planned to use the ports of Calais and Boulogne to take off the base personnel in the area. During Operation Dynamo some 765 British vessels of all types, including French, Belgian and Dutch vessels, were used to bring away the troops. Part of the Dunkirk myth was to ascribe a critical role to the small vessels, manned largely by amateur sailors – the reality was that the majority of the men (some 230,000) were taken off by destroyers from the East Mole (and the French from the West Mole); only some 100,000 were lifted directly from the beaches. The British continued to be fortunate in both weather and the inability of the Luftwaffe to interdict shipping between France and England. As a result only some 2,000 servicemen were lost in the passage of ships from Dunkirk.

Although preparations for evacuation and actual embarkation had continued from the 19th, Operation Dynamo itself commenced on the evening of Sunday, 26 May. Prior to this some 26,402 British and 1,534 Allied soldiers (largely base personnel) had already been evacuated. As Boulogne had fallen on the 25th to 2nd Panzer Division and resistance in Calais by 30 Brigade was ceasing on the 26th, the evacuation plans had to be adjusted to make use of Dunkirk.

Between 26 May and 4 June 338,226 British, French and Belgian soldiers were evacuated from Dunkirk.

Even on 30 May it was only expected that the defence of the Dunkirk perimeter could last only for another day or two, and plans were made for the evacuation of II Corps through I Corps, which would then be surrendered to the Germans (III Corps as a formation did not really exist any longer). In fact it became possible to evacuate almost all British troops, as the French took more and more responsibility for the Dunkirk perimeter defence. Although more than 120,000 French troops were also evacuated, perhaps as many as 40,000, including many who had formed a critical element of the final rearguard, were left behind.

As a result of the 'Dunkirk Miracle' the First British Expeditionary Force was largely saved, although most of its heavy weapons and transport was lost. However, this deliverance was bought at a heavy price to non-BEF units and some 140,000 British soldiers and airmen were still left in France south of the River Somme.

Among them were three major formations: the 51st Highland Division, 1st Armoured Division and the ad hoc Beauman Division. Even while the BEF was being recovered from the harbours and beaches of Dunkirk, the British Government decided to create a Second BEF. This Second BEF was to be created around the nucleus of British units which were still fighting south of the River Somme and would be reinforced by the addition of a second corps from the UK. The original idea was that these units would form part of the French defensive line along the River Somme (called the Weygand Line). Later as the front broke, their role was changed to become part of a 'redoubt' force based in and around Brittany.

CHAPTER 3

The Sacrifice of the 'Construction' Divisions and the Port Defenders

Despite its inglorious retreat and evacuation, the vast majority of the men of the BEF were saved to fight another day, although, having abandoned their vehicles, heavy weapons and huge stores of ammunition, the nine divisions of the BEF had little left with which to resist a serious German attack on the UK. It was to take many months before they could be re-equipped and years before they could master the ability to defeat experienced German forces. Nevertheless, it could have been much worse. The Dunkirk evacuation had given Britain a second chance and it was able to retreat to its island fortress with the core of its professional and reserve army. There it could rebuild its forces, without facing the dreadful dilemma of seeing that army in German captivity.

Remarkably, the BEF had suffered relatively few casualties in the immediate aftermath of moving forward to the River Dyle and then the first part of the retreat to Dunkirk, the pull-back to the Escaut. The CIGS, General Ironside, visited France and General Gort on 20 May, and on his return reported to the Cabinet that less than 500 men had been lost from the BEF 4 up to 20 May. This remarkably low figure confused the Cabinet who did not understand how such a large army could be forced to retreat with so few casualties. However, this low figure was quickly out of date as the subsequent defence of the Arras area and the Dunkirk perimeter (particularly in Belgium) did result in some very heavy casualties. This affected not just the British, but also their Belgian and French allies particularly, those

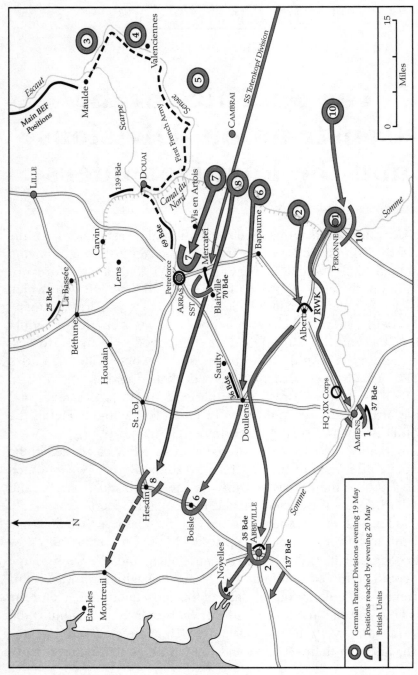

Map 2. Destruction of the Construction Divisions, 20 May 1940.

who held the Dunkirk perimeter in the final days of the evacuation.

Initially it was estimated that some 3,500 soldiers of the BEF and 1,500 RAF personnel were lost in the retreat, and perhaps another 2,000 men were lost in the sea evacuation. Set against the fact that some 230,000 British soldiers were saved to continue the defence of Britain, the loss of about 7,000 men seems a comparatively small price. Later it was estimated that total losses for the British (killed, wounded and captured) for the whole campaign, were actually some 68,000, of which almost half were killed or captured south of the River Somme in the fighting associated with the units of the Second BEF after Dunkirk.

Naturally Ironside's reported figure of 500 casualties was quickly rendered out of date, but it should also be borne in mind that this figure was just for the BEF itself, and ignored the fate of those very heavy casualties suffered in the unsuccessful attempts to plug the defences in the West and slow the advance of the German panzers. In comparison with the figures mentioned above, far more serious casualties were sustained by these other non-BEF units, whose fate has often been overlooked. On the 20th, the 51st Highland Division was moving out of the Maginot Line having withstood heavy German artillery and infantry attacks for ten days. By the time the real evacuation began on 26 May, over half of the eight brigades of construction troops as well as the Calais brigade had virtually ceased to exist. For example, the 7th Royal Sussex, which faced Rommel's 7th Panzer Division on the 20th near Amiens, had only seventy men left to be taken into captivity out of the 701 officers and men who entrained on 18 May from Normandy. Indeed the casualties suffered by these units (mostly on just one or two days in May) came close to the total Allied casualties of 13,560 that were suffered in the ten days of vicious fighting at El Alamein. Towards the close of his life, Montgomery stated that he was haunted by the heavy casualties suffered at Alamein – it is therefore appropriate to consider the sacrifice of the brave but unprepared men from the 'construction divisions'. In the official history, Major Ellis described the orders to join the battle which were sent to these men on 18 May as like setting out a 'few British pawns on the board'. He certainly did not conceal the sacrificial nature of the orders they received, although he thought that every hour of delay which they achieved for the BEF facing the German attacks in Belgium made the sacrifice worthwhile. Without denigrating the sacrifice of these men, it is extremely doubtful if the delays imposed by these brigades of infantry (sent into action with no supporting weapons and often with minimal transport) did very much to delay the progress of the seven German panzer divisions. Those who were there did not complain of their fate, but the reasons for these men being placed in their predicament is certainly worth recording in more detail.

As mentioned earlier, by March 1940 the French had mobilized over a hundred divisions, while Britain had only managed to increase the BEF in France to nine divisions. The French were distinctly unimpressed and the British decided to attempt to look more serious. As a token of its earnest intent, Britain offered to place the 51st Highland Division, a well-trained territorial division with an incredibly distinguished record from the First World War, at the disposal of the French for employment in the Maginot Line. The Division had landed in January 1940 and, having just completed its orientation training in France, was available to be used. The adventures of the Highlanders as they first defended the Maginot Line to the east of Thionville, and then met Rommel in Normandy, is told in Chapter 8.

As a further indication of their seriousness, the British decided at the same time to bring over three more infantry divisions from the UK. During the previous year a rapid expansion of the Territorial Army had been achieved by the simple expedient of splitting many units into two. With reinforcements the new battalions were brought up to strength, but there was little opportunity to give these men effective training as they were mainly used during the winter of 1939/40 as a guard force for vulnerable military targets in the UK.

For their employment in France, these twenty-six Territorial battalions, each of about 500-700 men, were formed into nominal brigades and divisions. However, unlike the brigades and divisions of the BEF, these formations had a minimal command and control structure, and the divisions were totally without artillery and anti-tank support. The individual units were equipped with only light local defence weapons, such as rifles, Bren light machine guns and a few Boyes .55 anti-tank rifles. They had very little transport of their own and their only support units were a number of signal and medical units, together with engineer field companies and field parks. This was entirely appropriate, given their role as basically labour units intended to expand the railways and base facilities of the rear areas of the BEF in France. Before sending these men to France, General Ironside, as CIGS, demanded a commitment from General Gort that these units would not be employed with the BEF until their training had been completed.

The three divisions (12th Eastern Division, 23rd Northumbrian Division and the 46th North Midland and West Riding Division) arrived in France in late April 1940. The 46th Division was committed to unloading ships, stacking ammunition and railway building around St Nazaire and Rennes in Brittany. The 12th Division was stationed in Normandy constructing railway lines and junctions at Rennes, and at the docks at Le Havre and Fécamp, while the 23rd Division was employed in the immediate rear area behind the BEF north of the River Somme, constructing airfields and access roads mostly around St Pol (which lies some 15 miles north-west of Arras). Although the men were on 'active service' in France, their work commitment meant there was still no real time or opportunity to continue their training, which had been rudimentary at best. Few considered this a serious problem as the men were located well to the rear and there existed no intention ever to use these soldiers in combat without serious training, incorporation into proper field units and the provision of appropriate support weapons.

However, the realization that the German panzer divisions were streaking to the west through areas largely devoid of troops, thereby cutting the BEF off from its bases and supplies, forced General Gort to throw these untrained men into a desperate bid to slow that advance.

On 16 May, General Georges, commanding all the Allied northern armies, realized that these armies were being outflanked by the stream of German armour heading west. He therefore requested

General Gort for the use of the 23rd Division to defend the line of the Canal du Nord, south of Arleaux. This canal runs virtually south to north from Péronne (on the River Somme) to Arleux, where it joins other canals to run to the sea at Gravelines and Dunkirk. The French had no other troops available to defend the Canal Line and Gort had no formed bodies of troops available from the BEF to defend it. At the time most of the BEF was located in northern Picardy and forward in Belgium around Brussels, while the rear areas were largely devoid of combat troops. Apart from Gort's two reserve divisions (5th and 50th), located in the rear of the BEF, his only other large body of troops was the three construction divisions, but he had already given a commitment not to use these largely untrained territorial soldiers until they had received adequate training and support. The German panzer divisions had already proven their ability to break through entrenched French infantry supported by the incredibly strong French artillery. He may have been desperate, but it must have been clear to him and his staff officers that calling forward unsupported, untrained riflemen to stop the hundreds of enemy panzers streaming west, supported by dive-bombers, artillery and mortars, would do little to stop the Germans and could only result in their deaths. Given the hopelessness of their situation, it is therefore quite appropriate to refer to their use as 'sacrificial'.

Nevertheless, Gort, faced by the lack of alternatives, felt compelled to send willing but untrained volunteers to try to stop the flood of armour heading west. Suddenly, men (mostly little more than young civilians in uniform) who had only been brought to France to make up working parties, were required to pick up their rifles and, often with no more than five rounds of ammunition each, attempt to stop columns of German panzers. It can certainly be asked if Gort should have even considered issuing these orders. Without doubt well-trained infantry equipped with the proper anti-tank weapons and tactics, and supported by artillery, can give a very good account of themselves against armour, but without those advantages they are condemned to be cut to pieces. Eventually some unit commanders recognized the futility of attempting to stop the panzers without the appropriate means of defence and withdrew their surviving troops to the coast where they were later evacuated.

Some of the units which attempted to defend built-up areas such as towns and villages were able to delay the panzers for anything up to eight hours, but those caught in the open had no chance. The issue was never in doubt and by the end of the day on 20 May, two Territorial divisions had been largely destroyed and the German panzers were at the Channel coast. The responsibility for this decision has been laid at the door of Gort, which is absolutely right since he was in command. However, it is quite possible that Gort, who was in Belgium conducting the main BEF battle from his minimal Advanced HQ at Renaux, may well have had very little to do with this decision. The actual decision to call the 'digging divisions' forward appears to have been taken on the 17th, in response to the request from General Georges, by Gort's principal staff officer at Rear GHQ, namely Lieutenant Colonel Robert Bridgeman. It was Bridgeman who actually ordered Major General Petre, the GOC of 12th Division, to come forward to Arras and take command of the ad hoc force which was to guard the rear of the BEF. The realization that the Germans had broken through and the French had no other troops to stop them came as something of a shock to Rear GHQ. Bridgeman's written order nevertheless suggested that only small detachments of Germans had penetrated the French defence lines, which were being rapidly strengthened. Anyway, in accordance with orders, trainloads of thousands of eager Territorials began to steam north from Normandy and Brittany on 18 and 19 May.

In any event, Rear GHQ under the command of the Adjutant General, Lieutenant General Sir Douglas Brownrigg demonstrated its confidence in the outcome of these measures by moving on the 17th and 18th from Arras to Boulogne. The French liaison officers with Rear GHQ were not informed of this panic move and it took them two days to find the location of the new Headquarters! When GHQ's accommodation in the Hotel Imperial was bombed on the 19th, it then moved to Wimereux (just east of Boulogne). After his meeting with General Billotte on the 19th, Gort seems to have been convinced that the French situation would leave the BEF with little alternative but to evacuate and he ordered Brownrigg to arrange to get rid of the 'useless mouths', including evacuating Rear GHQ to the UK. This significant evacuation was finally completed on 23 May, just as 2nd Panzer Division developed the second day of its attack on Boulogne. Bridgeman stayed on, as he had already begun planning how to extricate the rest of the BEF from the trap in France.

23RD NORTHUMBRIAN DIVISION

The closest construction units to the Canal Line were those of the 23rd Northumbrian Division which were based around St Pol. They had arrived in France in March and April of 1940 and were deployed in the area between St Pol and Bethune, where they were being used to construct airfields and access roads. The 23rd Division consisted of 69 and 70 Brigades, plus some divisional troops.

70 BRIGADE

The Brigade, with three battalions of the Durham Light Infantry (10th, 11th and 12th – the 12th was also known as the 1st Tyneside Scottish, later of the Black Watch), was based at Nuncq close to St Pol. Of the 2,000 men in the Brigade, 1,400 had never had the chance to complete their basic rifle training, yet this was considered to be one of the better-trained brigades. They were allocated to the defence of part of the Canal Line under Major General Petre (GOC 12th Division, who was to be based in Arras). However, these Territorial formations lacked not only support weapons but also command and communications system. As a result units found themselves without proper orders or intelligence about the enemy and without any means to locate or contact their superiors (who should have been looking for them!). Thus 36 Brigade, which was spread out on the roads leading north-west and west from Doullens to Arras, expected to be supported by units of 70 Brigade on its left flank, but 70 Brigade was never able to join them.

The men of 70 Brigade, under Brigadier Kirkup, had speedily moved forward from their base on 17 May, only to spend three days and nights marching and driving frustratingly around the area east of Arras. They had first gone to the Canal Line, which they discovered had virtually no water in it, and had begun preparing defensive positions and blowing bridges. They were then told to move back and head for Saulty south-west of Arras, to join a defensive line which had been established by 36 Brigade. They spent part of the night of 19/20 May at Neuville-Vitasse, before setting off for Saulty early the next morning. However, before reaching Saulty they were attacked by Germans around Ficheux and Blairville, south-west of Arras. Early on the morning of the 20th, the 11th DLI and the 1st Tyneside Scottish, under Lieutenant Colonel Swinburne, were caught in the open by reconnaissance units and companies of tanks from the 6th and 8th Panzer Divisions. The two battalions were cut to pieces, many were wounded and captured, and barely a few hundred survivors made their way back to the 10th Battalion, who were already further west at Beaumetz. Swinburne was captured and later estimated that 135 of his men and more than fifty others from the 11th DLI were killed, mainly by tank shells and machine guns. When the survivors stumbled into the 10th Battalion, its commanding officer, Lieutenant Colonel David Marley, decided to withdraw the remnants of the Brigade to north of the St Pol road. Eventually the survivors were evacuated through Dunkirk on 31 May.

69 Brigade

This brigade also set off on the 17th from its working bases, which were nearby to St Pol and Béthune. It consisted of the 5th Battalion, East Yorkshire Regiment and the 6th and 7th Battalions, Green Howards, and these were deployed along the natural defence line of the River Scarpe to defend Arras from the north. On 23 May, the 6th Green Howards, under Lieutenant Colonel Steel, were then sent north to Gravelines, to form part of the defence of the western approach to Dunkirk. At first they managed to hold out with the aid of some tanks for two days against attacks by 1st Panzer Division. At one stage they were ordered to make an infantry counter-attack, which resulted in heavy casualties. Then they were relieved and marched down to the beach where they expected to be able to embark for England. However, on the 29th, they were ordered to turn around and march back once again to confront enemy armour which was trying to make a breakthrough in the area of Bergues. After suffering more casualties the survivors were finally withdrawn to the beach and the remnants of the Battalion embarked on 1 June from Dunkirk.

The 8th Battalion, Northumberland Fusiliers, a motorcycle battalion from 23rd Division was also sent into Arras on the 20th to reinforce its defenders who, under the command of Major General Petre, were called Petreforce. Initially Petreforce consisted of little more than the 1st Battalion Welsh Guards, who moved into the town on 17 May and immediately started blocking the major roads into the town. They were then joined on the 20th by the 5th Green Howards from 150 Brigade of 50th Division. When the British tanks and infantry pulled back to the Canal Line after the 22nd, Arras was left sticking out like an appendix pointing south from the main Allied defensive positions on the Canal Line and River Scarpe. Arras was required as a base for further operations if the Allies were to strike south and link up with the bulk of French Army which lay south of the River Somme. However, after the British attack at Arras of the 21st, the Germans were equally determined to crush the town as a dangerous obstacle to their control of the area. A belated French attack by two divisions on the 22nd was easily contained by the Germans and they began to reduce Arras with their 11th Motorized Brigade. During the 23rd the garrison was told that it had to fight to the finish. However (when almost completely surrounded by the Germans), on the night of the 23rd/24th, Petreforce was finally ordered to evacuate Arras and rejoin the BEF.

12TH EASTERN DIVISION

The 12th Division was based further south in Normandy. On 17 May its commander, Major General Petre, was nominated to command the defence of the Canal Line north of Arras and Arras itself, which was also the location of the large headquarters known as the Rear GHQ of the BEF. He began to move up immediately and ordered elements of his 36 Brigade, which was partially motorized, up to the area of the Canal Line, where it left the River Somme, just about 25 miles south-east of Arras.

36 BRIGADE

All of the Territorial construction units had arrived in France without transport or artillery. However Brigadier Beauman, who commanded the northern sector of the British rear area, had issued some of the units of 36 Brigade with trucks in order to create a mobile capability for the defence of his widespread bases. Brigadier Beauman provided a good example of how a resourceful officer can make things happen – with his vehicles full of stores which were likely to fall into the hands of the Germans, he therefore decided it was better to issue the vehicles while there was time for them to be of use. As a result of his initiative, the 7th Battalion, Royal West Kents were issued with 3-ton trucks and also with four 25pdrs (which had come back to Base Workshops from 51st Highland Division, then serving in the Maginot Line).

He identified experienced artillery personnel who were able to fire the four guns that accompanied the 7th Royal West Kents and they all they drove rapidly up to the start of the Canal Line near Péronne on the 17th. They did not have to wait long before meeting the Germans. The 7th Royal West Kents repulsed a raid by German reconnaissance units on the bridge connecting Péronne with Cléry during the night of the 18th/19th. They then moved back to Louvencourt, just outside Albert, on the 19th, before being ordered to defend Albert itself early on the 20th, arriving shortly before the advance elements of 1st Panzer Division reached the town. The 7th Royal West Kents fought hard that morning, retreating through the burning buildings, but the 25pdrs quickly used up their allocation of ammunition and the rifles of the Royal West Kents could do little more against experienced infantry supported by artillery, tanks and Stukas. By 0900 hrs the battle was virtually over and Lieutenant Colonel Basil Clay, the Commanding Officer, ordered the survivors to withdraw, break into small groups and try to make it back to Doullens, about 15 miles away, where the rest of 36 Brigade were located. In the event, Clay and most of the survivors were captured. Only a party of about seventy men under Captain Newbury got away to Boulogne, where they were evacuated on the 23rd.

The headquarters and the rest of 36 Brigade had come up to

Doullens from Rouen by train on the 18th. They had set up road blocks on the roads leading in to Doullens, with the 5th Battalion, The Buffs covering a 6-mile arc on the left from Pommera to Saulty and the 6th Royal West Kents covering the eastern approaches to Doullens. The Brigade was under the command of Brigadier George Roupell VC, who established his headquarters in the chateau at Lucheux, just a few miles north-east of Doullens. Meanwhile, it was expected that units of 70 Brigade would move into the area to cover the open flank to the north around Saulty.

Two officers from the 7th Royal West Kent's battle in Albert made it back in time to warn the rest of 36 Brigade of the approaching panzers as two panzer divisions homed in on Doullens. 6th Panzer Division attacked the 5th Buffs at about 1315 hrs on the afternoon of 20 May, their line was quickly broken and the forward companies were cut off. The survivors made their way north and linked up with Brigadier Roupell, before making their way to Boulogne. Major Penlington got a party of sixty to Boulogne where they helped with the defence until being evacuated. Only some eighty survivors of the 5th Buffs got back to England.

2nd Panzer Division came down the Doullens Road and attacked the 6th Royal West Kents west of Doullens, just after midday. They were able to conduct a fighting withdrawal into Doullens, where they exploited the advantage of fighting armoured units in built-up areas, and their last strongpoint did not surrender until 2030. The survivors again broke up into small groups and attempted to evade capture (although few were successful).

In the actions at Albert and Doullens on 20 May, the two battalions of Royal West Kents lost over 1,000 men killed, wounded and captured. Only about fifty of the 6th Royal West Kents under Captain Nixon reached Boulogne and were evacuated to England on the 23rd. Another party under Captain Carr managed to get back to Rouen and were evacuated from Cherbourg on 7 June.

35 BRIGADE

The 2/5th Battalion, Queen's Royal Regiment was sent on 15 May to defend the airfields around Rambures, about 15 miles south-west of

Abbeville. On the 18th, the 2/6th and 2/7th Battalions, Queen's Royal Regiment were entrained and sent north to defend Abbeville, but no sooner had they arrived than they were ordered to travel to Lens, some 20 miles north of Arras. The destination seemed strange, but they checked the order with GHQ and it was confirmed. The two battalions then entrained again, finally arriving at Lens by 1900 hrs that evening. They were not expected at Lens and further calls to GHQ revealed that the order should have read 'Proceed Doullens', not 'Proceed to Lens'. Eventually the weary troops were gathered together, put back on trains and taken first to Arras where they spent the night. The next day they made their way back to Abbeville, where they met the 2/5th Battalion, which had marched from Rambures the previous day. The three battalions then set up defensive positions around Abbeville, mostly north of the Somme River. These battalions were hit at about 1630 on the 20th by the advance elements of the 2nd Panzer Division and were soon overcome. When the survivors were forced to escape across the River Somme, some of them drowned but most were captured. Out of an original brigade strength of 2,400, only 1,234 reached the Base Depot at Rouen on 23 May.

37 BRIGADE

Two of the battalions of 37 Brigade, the 6th and 7th Royal Sussex Regiment, were based near the great railway junction at Abancourt, where they were working on the extension of the rail facilities planned for the great expansion of the BEF, which was due to happen in 1941. The two battalions were then ordered to entrain on the 18th for Abbeville, but also received the corrupted message to proceed to Lens (rather than Doullens) and were on their way there when they suffered a German air attack at St Roche (just west of Amiens). This hit the two leading coaches of the train carrying the 7th Royal Sussex, including the officers' coach, and resulted in more than eighty casualties, many of the killed and wounded being officers. As a result, the Battalion detrained and the following day, in the absence of any new orders, set up defensive positions outside Amiens on some high ground on the Poix road. They were established by noon on the 20th, which was just in time to offer a vigorous defence to the

31

tanks of 1st Panzer Division. Given their limited weapons and ammunition, the outcome was never in doubt and by 2000 hrs only seventy survivors were left to be taken prisoner. This was a horrifying casualty rate for a battalion that had set out with 701 officers and men, just two days earlier.

The 6th Royal Sussex had been in a following train which, because of the track damage, was diverted into sidings at Amiens. Eventually it was diverted south of the Somme to Ailly-sur-Noye where it remained without any information or orders for two days before the Commanding Officer managed to get hold of a train which took them south to Paris. In Paris he managed to contact the British Military Attaché and finally got orders to travel to Blain, near Nantes in Brittany, where the Battalion stacked ammunition until it was evacuated on 17 June.

The third battalion, the 2/6th East Surreys, was equipped with transport to act as mobile reserve and was therefore ordered to travel from Rouen to Montreuil (the small port south of Boulogne) on 20 May in order to protect the sea flank of the BEF. It was joined for the journey by the 4th Buffs, a line-of-communication battalion, which had also been equipped with transport. However, as it drove north it was delayed by the streams of refugees hurrying south, and by the time it approached Abbeville, the town was already occupied by the Germans. The 2/6th East Surreys stopped in Fresseneville and the 4th Buffs in Le Translay, but as it was impossible to get across the Somme both battalions returned to the Le Tréport area. The 2/6th East Surreys were then used to replace the 4th Border Regiment who had been acting as the infantry screen for the Support Group of 1st Armoured Division. As such, the largest part of the 2/6th East Surreys were to share the fate of the 51st Highland Division in Normandy.

46TH (NORTH MIDLAND AND WEST RIDING) DIVISION

The 46th (North Midland and West Riding) Division was a full-strength Territorial division of nine infantry battalions grouped into three brigades, with a glorious history. During the First World War it had established a solid reputation as a fighting division from early in

1915 when it had been the first fully formed Territorial division to arrive in France. In the spring and summer of 1918 the Germans had launched a series of powerful attacks which drove huge salients into the Allies' fronts. However, having desperately held these strong German advances, the Allies began their counter-attacks in July and August, which recovered much of the lost ground. Although the German Army had shot its bolt, it was still a formidable adversary protected by deep defences on the Western Front, which the Germans had spent two years fortifying. Nevertheless, by the end of September 1918, the British Fourth Army had fought its way across the old Somme battlefields and was approaching the main German fixed-defence structures.

Fourth Army included the 46th Division, which was considered so experienced that it was given the task of cutting through the deep defences of the Hindenburg Line, which lay along both sides of the wide St Quentin Canal. Despite being faced by a heavily fortified canal, pillboxes filled with machine guns and deep defence bunkers, the 46th Division achieved a signal victory on the morning of 29 September. Remarkably, the men of the leading brigade, 137 Staffords' Brigade, wearing lifebelts requisitioned from Channel steamers, were able to swim the canal, take the village of Bellenglise and cut through the Hindenburg Line in less than six hours, with minimal casualties. The rest of the Division went on to take the village of Magny la Fosse, while the Bellicourt tunnel defences were captured by the 5th Australian and 30th American Divisions. Over 4,000 prisoners and seventy guns were captured by the Division. The British Fourth Army, by breaking through the Hindenburg Line so quickly, not only achieved a major victory, but brought forward the prospect of ending the War in 1918, and was able to push the damaged and retreating German Army back to the German border.

However in 1940, most of this hard-won experience had been lost and the Division was initially spread around the various dumps and bases in Brittany as little more than unskilled working parties. Therefore when Major General Curtis, the GOC of 46th Division, was ordered to take charge of holding the Canal Line from Watten to St Omer, it took a while to organize their grouping and transport up to

Béthune on the Canal Line. In addition to the troops of his own division, General Curtis was also given 25 Brigade (detached from 50th Division) plus ad hoc groups of men varying from RASC drivers to searchlight units. 25 Brigade, with its three infantry battalions and a field artillery regiment with some twenty-four guns, was allocated the centre of the line around La Bassée, as this was considered vital to maintain the communications with the troops in Arras, where GHQ was located. At best this grouping of units (initially called Polforce) was too dispersed to hope to offer much resistance to German forces once they turned north, but they were able to man most of the bridges over the rivers and canals and provide some security until reinforced a few days later by three BEF divisions (2nd, 44th and 48th) from the south.

The 2nd, 44th and 48th Divisions had been relieved on the eastern end of the Allied defence pocket by French and Belgian units on 23 May. At first it was intended that these troops would be used for the French attack south planned for 26 May. However, Gort was clearly never convinced that an attack south was a realistic prospect and he ordered these divisions to take up positions behind the western Canal Line to protect that flank on the 24th, by the occupation of strongpoints (mostly well behind the River Aa) from Bergues, Wormhout, Cassel, Hazebrouck and down to La Bassée. This repositioning and strengthening of the British defences benefited from the German decision not to advance across the Canal Line from 24 to 26 May (brought about by the famous 'Halt Order').

Initially General Curtis began organizing positions on the Canal Line from the 20th, utilizing his three brigades as they arrived in the area from Brittany. Two of the brigades got through by the morning of the 20th, but that afternoon, as four troop trains were approaching Abbeville from the south, the town came under attack from the advance elements of Guderian's Corps. In the first train were Brigadier Gawthorpe and the headquarters of his 137 Brigade, as well as the 2/5th Battalion, West Yorkshire Regiment. In the other three trains were the other two battalions of infantry from 137 Brigade, namely the 2/6th and 2/7th Battalions, Duke of Wellington's Regiment, and their two Royal Engineer squadrons. In the final train was the 2/4th Battalion, KOYLI from 138 Brigade.

137 BRIGADE

They had been on their way to Béthune from Rouen since the 18th, but their journey had been tortuous. As they travelled north they had found the track blocked by a panic demolition at Abancourt and they had had to return to Rouen, where they were diverted via Dieppe. However just as the four trains approached Abbeville on 20 May, along the coast railway line, they came under air attack from the Luftwaffe. An alert signalman switched the first train onto the track to Boulogne, but the other three trains were halted by the damaged track. Thus three battalions, sorely needed for the defence of the Canal Line, were stuck south of the River Somme, with no means of joining the BEF at Béthune. Abbeville was already occupied by the Germans, so after a reconnaissance the three battalions had no choice but to withdraw. It took them two days to march, on foot and with short rations, to Dieppe, which was still being used as a casualty clearing port.

Brigadier Beauman, the Northern Area Commander, decided to retain 2/7th Battalion, Duke of Wellington's Regiment as a garrison for Dieppe, and sent the 2/6th Battalion of the Dukes and the 2/4th Battalion, KOYLI, south to the reinforcement depots near Rouen. Eventually these two battalions were deployed in the defence of the River Seine crossings against new German attacks on the French Army south of the Somme, which commenced on 6 June. Both battalions suffered heavy casualties defending the bridges over the Seine before the remnants were evacuated from St Malo and Cherbourg on 17 June.

2/7th Duke of Wellington's remained at Dieppe, until the German attack across the River Somme, when it acted as a rearguard for the 51st Highland Division as it retreated from the River Bresle. On 11 June the Battalion arrived at the pretty village and harbour of Veules-les-Roses and established a defensive perimeter with the French just outside the village. It was then involved in very heavy fighting against Rommel's tanks in which three officers and sixty-two soldiers were killed. However, their sacrifice held the panzers back, and about half the Battalion managed to get away in the small ships which came in and evacuated survivors. In a quiet corner of the

35

communal cemetery of Veules-les-Roses remain some of the soldiers from the Battalion who heroically defended the evacuation of their comrades on the morning of 12 June.

So although actually only the 2/5th Battalion, West Yorkshire Regiment from 137 Brigade made it to the Canal Line, the remainder of the Brigade, south of the River Somme, were also heavily involved in trying to repel the German advances. The 2/5th West Yorkshires eventually helped defend St Omer. It was also at St Omer that the remnants of 8th Battalion, Royal Northumberland Fusiliers (a machine-gun battalion from 23rd Division), which had also been moved up to the Canal Line, lost its main support company in a German trap. After suffering many casualties due to bombing, the survivors of the 2/5th were evacuated from Dunkirk together with the survivors of the 5th Battalion, East Yorkshire Regiment, from 69 Brigade.

138 BRIGADE

The remaining two battalions of 138 Brigade, the 6th Battalion, Lincolnshire Regiment and 6th Battalion, York & Lancaster Regiment joined the defenders of the Canal Line and supported by the 16th and 53rd Field Regiments RA put up a vigorous defence of the southern flank of Dunkirk around Teteghems until 30 May. 138 Brigade then thinned out and was evacuated the next night.

139 BRIGADE

From 139 Brigade, the 2/5th Battalion, Leicestershire Regiment were installed along the River Scarpe near Douai. When they were attacked on the 24th by German panzers they suffered very heavy casualties, only the reserve company and some stragglers finding their way to Dunkirk and evacuation. 2/5th Battalion, Sherwood Foresters Regiment defended Oignies and the 9th Battalion of the same Regiment fought vigorously at Cassel. 139 Brigade, despite its heavy casualties, remained an important element of the defence by 46th Division and was gradually moved north. It was among the last defenders of Dunkirk holding the perimeter around Teteghems and Couderque until the night of 1/2 June, when the Brigade, as well as the headquarters of 46th Division and 1st Division, were finally ordered to move back to Dunkirk and evacuation.

46th Division, despite its limited resources, functioned as an active headquarters from 20 May until it was one of the last to be evacuated from Dunkirk. It had been responsible for defending a large part of the canal line from La Bassée to Raches and then along the Scarpe River from Raches to St Armand (and Millonfosse), as well as part of the Dunkirk perimeter. It had suffered many casualties but had vindicated its choice as an active headquarters for the defence of the rear of the BEF.

CHAPTER 4

The Defence of Boulogne

The realization that the Germans were drawing close to the Channel coast also forced the War Office to consider reinforcing the main British resupply ports of Boulogne and Calais. On 21 May, it ordered part of 20 Guards Brigade under Brigadier Fox-Pitt, to move to Dover and thence to Boulogne, which it reached on 22 May. The contingent consisted of the 2nd Battalion Irish Guards and 2nd Battalion Welsh Guards, together with the Brigade Anti-Tank Company and 275 Battery of the 69th Anti-Tank Regiment. They joined a contingent of eight 3.7-inch anti-aircraft guns and a searchlight battery, which had been sent out a week earlier. Already based in the town were some French defenders equipped with a small number of antiquated field guns. They were also joined by Lieutenant Colonel Dean and members of his AMPC pioneers, together with small parties from the 6th and 7th Royal West Kents and the 5th Buffs. These were the survivors of the gallant attempt by the 2,000 Territorials of 36 Brigade to stop 2nd Panzer Division in Albert, and 6th Panzer Division in Doullens, on 20 May. Equipped with just rifles and Bren guns they had managed to delay the panzers for a number of hours, but at a very heavy cost. Nevertheless, having evaded capture to reach Boulogne, these less than 200 survivors were delighted to join in the defence of the town against the approaching Germans.

The enemy, in the shape of the 2nd Panzer Division, reached Boulogne during the afternoon of 22 May. It had been commanded by General Guderian when it was first established at Würzburg in 1935 and later, when he became the Corps Commander of XVI Corps, he had taken 2nd Panzer Division to Vienna for the *Anschluss* of Austria in 1938. The Division remained in Vienna and received

Austrian replacements so that it eventually became known as the Vienna Division. In 1939, it took part in the invasion of southern Poland. Like each of the three divisions in Guderian's Corps, 2nd Panzer Division was a very formidable organization at this stage of the War. With its administrative tail it comprised some 14,000 men carried in 3,000 fighting and support vehicles. By comparison, later in the War every panzer division had a reduced establishment of just one tank regiment with three tank battalions, and many panzer divisions were sent into combat with scarcely 100 tanks. However, at the beginning of this Western campaign, Guderian stated that the ten German panzer divisions comprised thirty-five tank battalions containing a total of 2,574 tanks (although even this figure still appears to be remarkably small).

Apart from the 9th and the three so-called Light divisions (the 6th, 7th and 8th were described as Light because each had originally been intended to operate as quasi-cavalry, with just one tank regiment of three battalions, mainly equipped with Czech tanks, while the 9th Division had only two tank battalions), the other six main Panzer divisions each had a tank brigade of two tank regiments, both with two tank battalions at full strength. Most of these divisions crossed the border with more than 400 of the most modern Pz III and Pz IV medium tanks. The reliability of these tanks was extremely good and casualties fairly light, so that by the conclusion of the Somme campaign most divisions still had more than 60 per cent of their tanks ready for action, with an average of just 20 per cent destroyed in combat and 20 per cent in workshops (many with relatively short repair periods). 5th Panzer Division reported in its War Diary on 25 May that its losses were almost up to a third and it had been forced to amalgamate its four tank battalions into three. 7th Panzer Division, which had been driven even harder by Rommel, was forced to amalgamate its three battalions into just a single battalion. Guderian's theories of the value of firepower and movement were vindicated by the total figures reported for von Kluge's Fourth Army, which included five panzer and three motorized divisions. During the whole northern campaign, up until 30 May, it reported it had only lost 131 tanks of all types, and most of these were the lighter reconnaissance and outdated Pz I and II types. It had only lost eleven Pz IIIs and thirteen Pz IVs.

2nd Panzer Division's major fighting assets included more than its two regiments of tanks. In addition it had a rifle brigade of three battalions of motorized infantry (carried in lorries and armoured half-tracks), an armoured reconnaissance battalion equipped with motorcycles and armoured cars, an anti-tank battalion with some forty-two anti-tank guns, an anti-aircraft battalion with three batteries of light and heavy anti-aircraft guns, as well as an extremely effective combat engineer battalion which carried boats and bridging materials. In addition, the Division had its own artillery regiment with three battalions of field guns and howitzers. Each artillery battalion had three batteries of four guns, which provided the divisional artillery with the ability to shell an enemy with the combined fire of twelve heavy 150mm towed howitzers and another twenty-four lighter 105mm guns, which could also be used as howitzers. When pitted against fortifications, the panzer divisions had already discovered that they could also make very effective use of their nine heavy (88mm) anti-aircraft guns, firing high-explosive shells. Finally its air reconnaissance capability included nine spotter planes as well as being guaranteed close support by Luftwaffe bombers and dive-bombers.

2nd Panzer Division had suffered from damage and casualties, particularly at the crossing of the River Meuse, and breakdowns during the long approach march. Even so, by the time of its arrival at Abbeville on the evening of 20 May, it would still have had more than two thirds of its strength, which would have left more than 10,000 men and some 300 medium and light tanks to take on the few thousand defenders of Boulogne. 2nd Panzer had barely one day to regroup on the north bank of the River Somme and secure some of its bridges before Guderian sent it north, and the division was still very short of fuel. It set out early in the morning of 22 May from the area around Abbeville to drive the 60 kilometres to Boulogne, but it was held up by stiff French resistance in Samer just outside Boulogne. It was therefore not until 1700 hrs that it was able to launch a full-scale attack against the Irish Guards in the south-east of the town, but that attack was repulsed with heavy casualties. The next attack was launched later that evening against the Welsh Guards holding the north-eastern part of the perimeter defence, but once again the attack was beaten off. The Guards had the support of their anti-tank platoon, as well as some groups of Territorial soldiers who had survived the sacrificial attempt to stop the German drive to the west.

That night, General Veiel had to report his division's lack of success to Guderian. For the Germans attempting to surround the Allied armies in northern France, it was important not to allow Boulogne to be used as a resupply conduit, so for his attack next morning General Veiel was reinforced with all of XIX Corps' heavy artillery, which took up positions on the high ground outside the town. The attack opened early the following morning with a tremendous artillery barrage, which could be seen from England. Later in the day the Luftwaffe joined in bombing the town and shipping around Boulogne, but suffered eight aircraft downed from anti-aircraft fire and Royal Air Force fighters from England. Even more effective was the fire from Royal Navy ships close offshore, on German tanks and artillery positions. Nevertheless, the heavy shelling and casualties caused Brigadier Fox-Pitt to draw his defenders closer in around the ancient citadel of Boulogne, and to commence the destruction of the port facilities. At 1800 that evening the War Office sent an order that 20 Guards Brigade was to be evacuated immediately.

Accordingly, the Royal Navy sent in a succession of destroyers that evening to lift the troops. Royal Navy destroyers repeatedly steamed into the harbour engaging German tanks and machine guns, despite suffering great damage and casualties from close-range fire, and some 3,000 soldiers were evacuated by the *Witshed, Vimiera, Wild Swan* and *Venomous*. Not everyone had received the order to evacuate and when firing by the defenders continued on the 24th, destroyers were again sent in, including HMS *Windsor*, to pick up more survivors. The last British and French defenders who held out around the Citadel surrendered on 25 May. Altogether more than 500 British soldiers were captured in Boulogne, while some 6,000 French soldiers under General Lanquetot also surrendered.

The decision by the War Office to evacuate 20 Guards Brigade as early as 23 May is difficult to fathom. The Guards had been sent to prevent Boulogne from falling into the hands of the Germans, which they were doing perfectly effectively until ordered to withdraw, thus leaving 2nd Panzer Division free to move on to the other channel ports. In fact, as not all the defenders received the order to withdraw, the continued resistance by those gallant men who had been left behind by their commanders continued to tie down 2nd Panzer Division, thereby forcing it to stay in the area, mopping up defenders for days, as a result of which it took only a very limited part in the general attack on the BEF. Guderian, who later downplayed the significance of the defence of the Channel Ports, reported that on 26 May some doughty British defenders opened fire on Sepp Dietrich, commander of the SS Leibstandarte Adolf Hitler Regiment, forcing him to go to ground and cover himself with wet mud to avoid being burnt by flaming petrol escaping from his damaged staff car. In fact, these troops were not Boulogne defenders but part of the 48th Division, which was deployed from Hazebrouck to Bergues to defend the BEF's retreat corridor to Dunkirk. The actual units involved in shooting up Dietrich's car appear to have been gunners from the Worcestershire Yeomanry and infantry of the 2nd Battalion, Royal Warwicks. In the end, Dietrich was forced to seek cover for almost six hours and eventually he had to be rescued by a number of bloody attacks by several tank platoons of the 2nd Panzer Division's 3rd Panzer Regiment.

Guderian states that on his return, he and his officers chaffed the discomforted Dietrich good-humouredly for getting himself into such a mess at Wormhout. Dietrich, however, was a well-known thug and the later gallant defence of Wormhout by the Royal Warwicks, Cheshires and others had its unhappy consequences. The SS troops appear to have received orders not to take prisoners and this resulted in a number of infamous massacres of dozens of British prisoners after their surrender. One of the worst incidents was at Le Paradis on 27 May, while in another the next day, soldiers from the 2nd Battalion of the Leibstandarte, under the command of

Hauptsturmführer Wilhelm Mohnke, gathered some eighty soldiers from the Royal Warwickshire Regiment, the Cheshire Regiment and Royal Artillery (all part of 48th Division), who had surrendered, and took them to a barn a short distance from Wormhout. The SS then threw stick grenades into the barn which killed and wounded many. Others were brought out of the barn in groups of five and shot. Mohnke was never arraigned for his crimes.

Clearly the resistance around Boulogne was a severe irritant to the Germans as it tied up one of their best panzer divisions and was certainly not the walkover claimed by Guderian. Nevertheless, following the main Boulogne evacuation on the 23rd, Guderian was free to redeploy his Corps heavy artillery against the defenders of Calais.

CHAPTER 5

The Defence of Calais

The defence of the Channel Ports had been placed directly under the CIGS and the War Office, which was, and still remains (in its present form), a totally unsuitable organization to run any battle or operation. Although Churchill reported that he approved the decision to evacuate Boulogne, it was probably a decision which he had seen but was unable to pay it sufficient attention. The order for the premature evacuation of Boulogne lacked strategic sense and was given without any consultation with the French forces in the area (who were not slow to complain). Churchill conveyed his disenchantment with this decision quite succinctly in his memoirs: 'I regretted our evacuation.' Churchill of all people recognized the importance of defending the Channel Ports area for British forces and decided that he had to take a firmer grip of the situation.

In August 1914, he, as First Lord of the Admiralty, had played a little-known but significant role in the outcome of the First Battle of the Marne, by sending a Marine brigade to the Channel Ports, which, while it achieved very little in military terms, had significantly distracted the German High Command, which feared the landing of fresh troops from England on that open flank. The landing of two British brigades at Boulogne and Calais in May 1940 illustrated the strategic flexibility open to the British, due to their abundant sea power. An operation to land the Canadian Division to support the British evacuation was also considered. In May 1940, Churchill feared that the Germans wanted to occupy all the French Channel Ports to prevent an escape by sea of British forces. Actually, the Germans had no idea (nor indeed did the French) that the British were thinking of evacuation – their prime concern was still to prevent the landing of further troops and supplies to support a breakout operation to the south by the British and French armies. Guderian's Corps Order No. 13 of the 25th makes it clear that once the coastal fortifications were captured they were to be manned and defended by the Germans themselves: 'Coastal Front ... is to be guarded and enemy landings prevented. The coastal defence installations already in existence are to be made ready for repelling attacks from seawards.'

The evacuation of Boulogne had proceeded so speedily that many British troops were not informed, including a company of the Welsh Guards who were left behind. Nor were the French defenders of the port under General Lanquetot holding out around the Citadel. As a result, General Lanquetot complained bitterly to the French Area Commander, Admiral Abriel in Dunkirk, who in turn complained to the French Government. Such a swift evacuation in the face of a strong enemy force was hardly evidence of the unstinting British support that Churchill was promising. As a result, Churchill responded to French complaints by countermanding the original evacuation instructions to the defenders of Calais, before giving orders that the planned evacuation of Calais, scheduled for 24 May, should not take place. Brigadier Nicholson and his 30 Brigade were to continue to defend Calais to the bitter end.

30 Brigade was another scratch formation formed in response to an emergency, having been formed at short notice from two crack infantry battalions (the Rifle Brigade and the KRRC), which had already been detached from the Support Group of 1st Armoured Division for special training in early May. These units were eventually sent on 23 May to Calais, where they were joined by the fine London Territorial Regiment, Queen Victoria's Rifles, and 3rd Royal Tank Regiment (also from 1st Armoured Division). Under Brigadier Nicholson, this force, supported by some Belgian and French soldiers, held out for more than three days against the fierce attacks of 1st and 10th Panzer Divisions.

In his memoirs, Heinz Guderian conveyed the impression that his three panzer divisions swept almost effortlessly up the Channel coast from the Abbeville area, and could easily have continued the offensive by moving north on 21 May, before a serious British defence was in place. He cited the interference from his Higher Command on the 17th, a lack of orders on the 21st, and the infamous (and to him unnecessary) 'halt order' of 24-26 May for delaying the deployment of his three divisions to take Boulogne and Calais, and reach the Dunkirk beaches before the British could begin their evacuation. Indeed, it was precisely this successful British evacuation which he blamed for the eventual loss of the War. He was almost certainly right about the consequences of the evacuation, which did allow Britain the opportunity to recover from its defeat and to rebuild its forces so it was able to defend itself against the overwhelming German forces gathering in northern France. However, in claiming that he could have swept up the British before their evacuation, he employed a substantial dose of post-event wisdom. In fact, by the 21st his divisions were very tired and short of supplies – they had experienced a long difficult approach march to the Meuse crossings and had then been in combat for more than ten days. Certainly Guderian's instinct was to take risks and keep urging on his troops (who nicknamed him 'Hurry on Fritz'), thereby keeping the enemy off balance, but there were many reasons why he could not have done as he claimed.

While it is true that the British and French had relatively few troops on the western side of Dunkirk until the third week in May, the French coastal defences were manned, there were garrisons in the main ports and these were quickly reinforced by the British from Britain. In addition, General Gort threw his three 'construction' divisions into the defence of the Canal Line and into the attempt to stem the advance of the seven panzer divisions from Army Group A, which threatened his rear. Although many units were completely outclassed and were consequently sacrificed, they did cause some delay to German movements, and those which actually got to the Canal Line remained a potent element of the defence force until evacuated. Furthermore, other ad hoc formations were quickly formed to defend the Canal Line and a stiffening defence was gradually put in place. As a result, the German panzer advance on the Dunkirk pocket defenders, although it eventually amounted to most of the panzer divisions, plus motorized and marching infantry, made comparatively slow progress, particularly in comparison to the speed of the race to the sea which had preceded it. Between the sea coast and the town of Douai, no less than ten divisions, half of them panzer, were committed against the Canal Line defenders. For example, Guderian reports that 1st Panzer Division commenced its attack against Gravelines and the Canal Line on 23 May. From the 26th, its attack was reinforced by 20th Motorized Division, the GrossDeutschland Regiment and the SS Division Leibstandarte Adolf Hitler, as well as by some elements from 2nd Panzer Division and XIX Corps artillery. This was an attacking strength of more than four strong divisions on a frontage of less than 10 miles. Gravelines was finally taken by 1st Panzer Division on the 29th, just before it was relieved to move south for the forthcoming attack against the French Army south of the Somme. The slow progress achieved by the Germans was a tribute to the sacrifice of the Calais defenders, as well as to those British and French units which conducted such a stubborn defence of the western approaches to Dunkirk.

Guderian made other contentious claims in his memoirs, such as the statement that von Rundstedt had nothing to do with the 'halt order' and that: 'As the commander on the spot, I am able … to state … that the heroic defence of Calais, although worthy of the highest praise, yet had no influence on the development of events outside Dunkirk.' The incontrovertible evidence which has now emerged is that the order to 'halt' came first from von Rundstedt's headquarters, before it was confirmed by Hitler. Furthermore, while it is certainly true that the order meant that those of his troops not directly involved with Calais or Boulogne were not hindered by the battle for these ports, they nevertheless made such slow progress after the order was lifted on the 26th, that they would clearly have benefited from the greater availability of Corps artillery and of the two panzer divisions, which remained partially tied up in those ports. Certainly, after the 26th, the Germans did not feel that time was a pressing issue since they knew they had the Allies completely surrounded by superior forces – but timing was clearly important. The slow pace of German progress mentioned above is a validation of the hard fighting by the defenders of the ports and the western approaches to Dunkirk. It was only when the 'halt order' was lifted that Calais finally surrendered on the evening of Sunday, 26 May, and Operation Dynamo began to lift the main body of the BEF from Dunkirk.

CHAPTER 6

The Defence of Arras and the Arras Attack

Arras was a small but important garrison city lying athwart the main German lines of communication to the coast. Its dogged defence became a significant factor in slowing the German assault on the defenders of the Dunkirk pocket and its approaches, due partly to the effect on the German Command of the stiff resistance provided by minimal British forces based in Arras, and to the combined sortie by British infantry and tanks, which shocked and interrupted the flow of at least two of the German divisions moving around Arras. The effectiveness of the Arras attack showed what might have been achieved south of the River Somme if the British forces had been organized as an independent entity.

Guderian's troops had met increasing resistance as they fought their way to the coast, which the first units (Colonel Spitta's battalion of 2nd Panzer Division) only reached late on the evening of the 20th. On 21 May, XIX Corps units were still securing the River Somme crossings and closing up to the Channel area. It was on this day that the British counter-attack from Arras was launched which, although poorly supported, met with such success that the SS Totenkopf Division was severely shaken and Rommel's 7th Panzer Division reported that it had been attacked by five enemy divisions. In retrospect, Guderian's tactic of continuing to charge ahead without concern for his flanks was hugely risky, but was so successful that it is often not recognized for the very vulnerable thrust it actually was. Guderian believed, and indeed repeatedly practised the creed, that fast-moving, hard-hitting panzer troops could so unbalance an enemy's command structure that even severely outnumbered

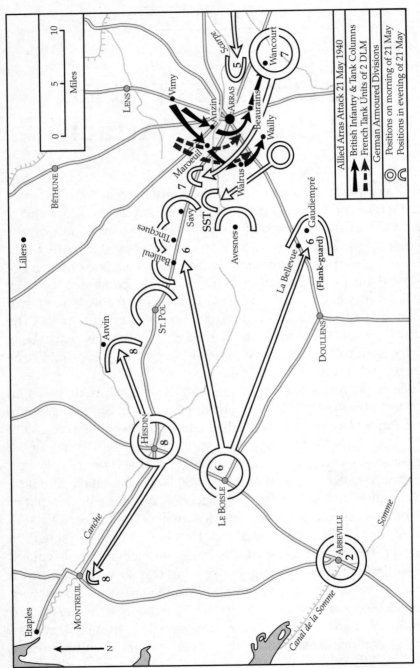

Map 3. The Arras Attack, 21 May 1940.

Allied Arras Attack 21 May 1940

British Infantry & Tank Columns
French Tank Units of 2 DLM

German Armoured Divisions
Positions on morning of 21 May
Positions in evening of 21 May

0   5   10
Miles

Wancourt 7
Scarpe
5
Vimy
Anzin
ARRAS
Beaurains
Wailly
Maroeuil
Walrus
7
Savy
SST
Tincques
Bailleul
6
Avesnes
Gaudiempré
6
La Bellevue
(Flank-guard)
LENS
BÉTHUNE
Lillers
Anvin
St. Pol
8
HESDIN
8
DOULLENS
LE BOISLE
6
Canche
MONTREUIL
8
Étaples
ABBEVILLE
2
Somme
Canal de la Somme
N

THE DEFENCE OF ARRAS AND THE ARRAS ATTACK

armoured troops, used in the right way, could take on and defeat far larger forces. To some extent this same principle was also validated by General O'Connor's employment of small numbers of British armour to operate so successfully against much larger, but largely static, Italian forces in the Libyan Desert in 1940-1.

The German senior commanders, who were well aware of the vulnerability of their long open flanks, were alarmed and with good reason. The Arras attack was precisely the Allied response which the senior German commanders most feared, as a strong pincer attack from the north and south could easily have cut off the leading German panzer divisions from their supplies, and could perhaps have led to their encirclement and destruction. In any event General Guderian was affected by the ensuing caution and wrote that:

> A noteworthy event occurred to the north of us: English tanks attempted to break through in the direction of Paris. At Arras they came up against the SS Division Totenkopf, which had not been in action before and which showed signs of panic. The English did not succeed … but they made a considerable impression on the staff of Panzer Group von Kleist, which suddenly became remarkably nervous.

The Arras attack should have been a combined armour and infantry operation delivered by two British divisions supported by two French divisions, including strong armoured elements. As such it could have seriously threatened the German panzer thrusts and indeed might have been enough to cause their withdrawal from the coast. In the event, the attack was put together with just two Territorial battalions of the Durham Light Infantry (DLI) from 50th Division, supported by two Royal Tank Regiment (RTR) battalions with just seventy-four tanks. For part of the action they were also supported by elements of a French light armoured division (3rd DLM) with another sixty Somua tanks (20-ton heavily armoured tanks with a 47mm gun).

The fact that the impact on the Germans was out of all proportion to the troops involved illustrates only too clearly the value of surprising and unbalancing the enemy. It showed what the Allies could have achieved with proper co-ordination between their armies as well as between infantry, tanks and artillery. It was hoped to do

53

precisely this with the British and French troops available south of the River Somme, and for that reason it is worth looking at the Arras operation in some detail.

It is an interesting historical fact that the commanders of the BEF in 1914 and 1940 behaved remarkably similarly. Separated by more than twenty-five years, Lord Gort in 1940, and Sir John French in 1914 experienced similar frustrations as they attempted to avoid losing Britain's only army in an European adventure. Both suffered from an inability to communicate with their French allies and felt that they had been left exposed by the action of the French armies on their flanks, forcing them into premature retreats. So within days of combat commencing they had both decided that they needed to withdraw their precious troops from the action to reform their forces. In the case of Sir John French, he was summoned to Paris by Lord Kitchener on 1 September 1914 and told in uncompromising terms that he had to co-operate with the French. In May 1940, the British had moved forward to the River Dyle from their prepared defences on the French border. For the first five days nothing very much had happened in front of the British positions on the Dyle. However, as the main German attacks fell on the French and Belgian armies on the BEF's flanks, Gort was forced to pull back from the Dyle successively to the river lines of the Senne, Dender and the Escaut. Thus, within nine days of the German attack beginning, he was in full retreat and began eying the Channel Ports, while his staff began contingency planning for the use of Dunkirk for resupply and back-loading of superfluous personnel.

Realizing that the Allies had been outflanked by the panzers' advance from Sedan to Abbeville, Gamelin suggested a plan for the combined Allied armies to counter-attack south, cutting through the panzer support lines and joining up with the main French Army south of the Somme. Remote from the fighting in London, the British Cabinet supported Gamelin's plan and on 19 May, dismayed at hearing Gort was considering a forced withdrawal to Dunkirk, the Cabinet ordered him to march south into France. Gort rejected Gamelin's plan as impracticable because he already realized the total impossibility of the BEF (largely intact but already short of rations and ammunition), as well as the French First and Seventh Armies, being able to turn and strike south at right angles to their positions on the River Escaut in Belgium (while under fierce attack from strong German ground and air forces from the east). By marching south the BEF would have lost whatever air cover and resupply possibilities it had from the UK. Furthermore, this march south would have exposed Gort's flanks and involved either leaving the Belgian Army to fight the Germans alone or required the Belgians to leave Belgium! Nevertheless, Winston Churchill was determined to maintain French morale and pressed for offensive action to cut off the head of the German advance.

However Gort, faced with the realities of command, remained unenthusiastic and had, as mentioned already, rejected a similar proposal from General Billotte, commanding the French First Group of Armies, on the 19th. In the meantime, Gamelin had been sacked on the 18th and there now existed a leadership and power vacuum. Gort was convinced that the Germans had already advanced too far west to be stopped. He had by this time committed the three construction divisions in a desperate attempt to bolster French defences along the southern part of the Escaut and Canal lines. However, in conference with Ironside (who had travelled overnight to meet him at Wahagnies) on the morning of the 20th, he agreed to order General Franklyn to attempt to establish a bridgehead south of Arras using the BEF's two reserve divisions and its only tank brigade. It was anticipated that this force would be supported by two French divisions. Ironside then went with General Pownall (Gort's Chief of Staff) to liaise with General Billotte and General Blanchard, commanding First Army. Billotte was in a state of nervous exhaustion and at the meeting Ironside, a large man, grasped him by his tunic and shook him! Amongst many misunderstandings, the French were not convinced that the BEF would support a combined attack led by the French and were reluctant to support a British operation. Finally, the reluctant Billotte agreed to authorize an attack towards Cambrai by General René Altmayer's V Corps. In the event, Altmayer was also exhausted and unenthusiastic. Although at first he agreed to co-operate with Major General Franklyn, he then admitted that it was impossible to have one of his divisions (the 25th Motorized) in place before the 22nd. The best he could offer was to arrange cover for the western flank of the proposed attack by General Prioux's 3rd DLM (Light Armoured Division).

Time was of the essence if the attack was to take advantage of the gap between the leading panzer elements and the follow-on troops. Gort therefore decided that the attack by the two British reserve divisions should go ahead on the 21st, even though he was unable to arrange air cover. Major General Franklyn (commanding 5th Division) who had been appointed to command this two-divisional attack, supported by a brigade of tanks, was given the objective of relieving the pressure on Arras by clearing the area of German troops and extending the British defensive line as far south as the Cojeul and Sensée rivers.

The armour and the two reserve divisions (the 5th and the 50th) gathered around Vimy during the day and night of the 20th. General Franklyn gave his orders at 0600 hrs on the 21st and carried out a brief reconnaissance with Major General Martel (commanding 50th Division), who was appointed to command the actual attack. However, many elements were unfavourable for the success of this operation. The men of the Tank Brigade were keen to get to grips with the Germans, but their tanks were worn out, having just returned from a wild goose chase to Brussels and back. The tanks had taken five days to drive back some 120 miles along congested roads and desperately needed maintenance. The Tank Brigade actually comprised only two battalions (the 4th and 7th RTR). Of its original 100 medium tanks, only seventy-four were ready for action (plus twelve light tanks). The majority of these seventy-four slow but heavily armoured 'Infantry' tanks were the 10-ton Mark I tank equipped with a single machine gun. Only sixteen of the tanks were 25-ton Mark II Matilda tanks equipped with machine guns and a 2-pounder gun, which could hope to match the German main battle tanks and anti-tank guns on an equal basis. In other words, the British were planning to commit not much more than a company of medium tanks against at least two panzer divisions, although, of course, as their intelligence was minimal, they had little idea of the overwhelming odds they actually faced. As they ventured into the unknown they also lacked reliable maps and their radio batteries were flat.

A normal BEF division had three brigades each of three infantry battalions, but the BEF's two reserve divisions had only two brigades each. 50th Division had already lost 25 Brigade, which had been sent north to hold the Canal Line under General Curtis. General Martel was an enthusiastic supporter of the use of tanks and his writings had, amongst others, inspired Guderian to develop his tank organization and tactics. Therefore Martel planned to combine his small tank force with infantry and supporting artillery in a bold and imaginative plan to strike the Germans with a hard-hitting attack. However, as he organized his infantry for the attack he found that far from having available even twelve battalions in four brigades, he was reduced to just one brigade of three battalions. The deteriorating military situation required that the other three brigades, together with artillery and anti-tank units, were taken away to defend Arras from other German attacks.

13 Brigade was sent to relieve the French 23rd Division to the east of Arras on the River Scarpe, to allow the French to join in the attack. This at least promised the availability of French tanks to cover the British open flank. 150 Brigade was sent to strengthen the Arras garrison east of the town along the River Scarpe and 17 Brigade was held in reserve until the first phase of the operation was completed. Martel was therefore left with just Brigadier Churchill's 151 Brigade, comprising the 6th, 8th and 9th Battalions of the Durham Light Infantry, available for this so-called clearing-up operation, and even then, one battalion of the DLI was held back in reserve.

The Durhams were doughty Territorial soldiers who, like the two DLI battalions (the 10th and 11th) destroyed the day before by the panzers at Beaumetz, were ready to give a good account of themselves. However, like many Territorial units they had received very limited training and were poorly equipped with limited quantities of ammunition, support weapons and transport, and no radios; their supply position was no better. Men of the 6th Battalion had to milk some cows to provide tea for breakfast that morning before they could move off to the line of departure. The 8th Battalion had no food at all that day. The Durhams had bivouacked beside the great Canadian memorial at Vimy on the night of the 20th and because they lacked transport they had to march 15 kilometres to reach the assembly area for the tanks; they accordingly arrived footsore, hungry and late.

Martel's concept of operations was to advance with two columns of two combat teams, each composed of a battalion of tanks and a battalion of infantry, closely supported by artillery, anti-tank guns and with motorcycle scouts from the 4th Royal Northumberland Fusiliers. Each column would move south from the Arras–St Pol road along two parallel routes which ran around the western side of Arras, clearing whatever enemy forces it found until it reached the first objective of the River Cojeul, before establishing a defensive perimeter on its second objective, the River Sensée. The intention was that 17 Brigade, which had been held in reserve until the first phase of the operation was completed, would then move south around the eastern side of Arras to join them.

However, to call the eventual organisations combat teams (as the American Major Thompson did in his 1941 account) is to imbue these organizations with capabilities they did not possess. Unlike German panzer units, they had never worked or trained together before and had very limited means of communication (relying mainly on runners, flags or despatch riders). Guderian had spent years practising and developing the skills of infantry/tank co-operation, meshing this in with mobile reconnaissance and anti-tank and artillery fire plans, until these became firm battle drills. The British infantry had virtually no transport and could only march some distance behind the tanks (the tanks were pretty slow with top speeds of 10 or 18 mph, but were faster than the exhausted infantry). It was not clear who was commanding each column (nominally the infantry battalion commanders were placed in command, but this was resented by the tanks, which were in any case quickly out of contact) and the battalion commanders did not have the means to control the action or decide how they should co-operate. Brigadier Pratt, commanding the Tank Brigade, saw that a shambles was developing and asked General Martel to postpone the attack. However, for Martel this was an all-too-rare opportunity to test some of his theories of infantry/tank co-operation and it was too precious to be thrown away.

The columns were organized as follows:

Eastern Column started from Maroeuill

4th Royal Tank Regiment

8th Durham Light Infantry

365 Battery, 92nd Field regiment RA
(with 18-pounders)

260 Battery, 65th Anti-Tank Regiment RA

Western Column started from Ecurie

7th Royal Tank Regiment

6th Durham Light Infantry

368 Battery, 92nd Field Regiment RA*
(with 25-pounders)

206 Battery, 52nd Anti-Tank Regt RA

In fact, 368 Battery was unable to reach the start line in time to join the action.

In addition, each column had one platoon from 151 Brigade Anti-Tank Company and one scout platoon of the 4th Royal Northumberland Fusiliers on motorcycles. As 4th RTR only had Mark I tanks it was lent two troops (seven tanks) of the heavier Mark IIs from 7th RTR for this operation.

Having waited for the infantry to arrive (who were late) and then the French tanks (which did not arrive) the British tanks were finally ordered to move off at 1430 hrs on a very hot sunny afternoon. As it was thought that 70 Brigade held the road from Arras to Doullens, they expected to have a fairly clear route until they reached the area south of Arras, which was close to the area where (apparently unknown to them) most of 70 Brigade, under Brigadier Kirkup, had actually been ambushed the previous day.

They soon discovered that, far from making good progress along a clear route, there was no shortage of opposition or targets among enemy troops moving through the area. Both columns of tanks advanced with two squadrons up and quickly ran into enemy formations including vulnerable lorry-borne infantry. Both of the Infantry Tank types were largely impervious to the German 37mm anti-tank guns and either shot them up or ran them over. The other tank types (the A39 or the scout cars) were much softer targets and suffered accordingly.

The eastern column started from Maroeuill at 1430 and attacked Duisans with French tanks moving up on their right; a number of German prisoners were taken. Two companies of the 8th DLI and two troops of 260 Anti-Tank Battery were left to hold Duisans and look after the prisoners. The rest of the column moved off to the village of Warlus where more German troops were found. As the village was cleared, more prisoners were captured. Berneville was then taken and some of the 8th DLI and 7th RTR moved on towards the Doullens road where they clashed with the German 7th Panzer Division and the SS Totenkopf. With the British held up by artillery fire and air attack, and forced to withdraw to Warlus, the Germans then began to attack Warlus and Duisans.

The western column started from Ecurie and quickly occupied Dainville, Achicourt, Agny and Beaurains, with a small party reaching Wancourt. 4th RTR, holding the high ground south of Doullens, fought the German 6th Infantry Regiment all afternoon with heavy losses on both sides. German artillery operating from Telegraph Hill near Mercatel prevented them from advancing any further.

Both columns ran out of momentum against strong German forces and in the early evening, with no possibility of support or of reaching even their first objective, they were ordered to withdraw. Both tank battalion commanding officers were killed and the two battalions were so depleted that they had to be amalgamated for the rest of their time in France.

An important development in this battle was that the British tanks had come up against General Rommel personally, who was returning to look for his 7th Rifle Regiment, found the 6th instead and travelled with them to Wailly, where his tank came under fire and he came across fleeing Germans troops, mainly from SS Totenkopf. Realizing that he was facing a dangerous attack he took personal charge of the guns of his 78th Field Artillery Regiment which he directed to fire at the British tanks which were clearly impervious to normal anti-tank fire. Rommel recorded that his adjutant, Lieutenant Most, was killed at his side as he directed the fire of his 105mm and 88mm anti-aircraft guns. This, together with the Stuka attacks he ordered, forced the British back and the survivors eventually withdrew to Vimy Ridge during the night.

Nevertheless the results were quite spectacular. 7th Panzer Division reported losses that day of eighty-nine killed, 116 wounded and 173 missing. Totenkopf reported nineteen killed, two wounded and twenty-seven missing. Rommel himself reported that he had been attacked by elements of five divisions. Von Rundstedt wrote:

A critical moment came just as my forces reached the Channel. It was caused by a British counter-stroke southwards from Arras on 21st May. For a short time it was feared that the panzer divisions would be cut off before the infantry divisions could come up to support them. None of the French counter-strokes carried the threat of this one.

As mentioned earlier, this experience induced a certain cautiousness in the German commanders, resulting in their retaining 10th Panzer Division in the Abbeville area for an extra twenty-four hours and later issuing the 'halt order' which proved so beneficial to the Allied defenders around Dunkirk.

Despite Guderian's casual reference to the effect of the British attack on SS Totenkopf, he was significantly affected by the Arras attack. In his memoirs he was able to magnify his prescience by claiming that on 22 May, he intended to use two of his divisions to advance on Boulogne and Calais, while 10th Panzer Division was to attack towards Dunkirk via St Omer. The reality was that his boss, General von Kleist, was concerned to maintain a strong presence in the Somme area and ordered 10th Panzer Division to remain in

Group Reserve on that day. He also gave explicit orders that XIX Corps should attack Boulogne and XLI Corps (Reinhardt's Corps) should attack Calais. Kleist's objective was to ensure that the two corps should continue to cut off the BEF from its supplies and use their artillery to engage the port harbours, thereby preventing the British from using the ports for resupply, rather than entangling his tank units in built-up areas. Von Kleist makes this division of responsibility quite clear by allocating an inter-corps boundary running from Hesdin north-west to Marquise i.e. midway between Boulogne and Calais. His concern for his open flank to the east (towards the BEF and Dunkirk) is shown by his allocation of the SS Verfägungs Division to XLI Corps with responsibility for this open flank. Only on the evening of the 22nd, after XLI Corps was held up near St Omer, did von Kleist return 10th Panzer Division to XIX Corps and swing the inter-corps boundary so that Guderian's Corps could engage Calais and take responsibility for the Aa crossings up to Gravelines. To support his operations Guderian was also given 20th Motorized Infantry Division and the SS Leibstandarte Adolf Hitler Regiment.

Guderian was determined to maintain the forward momentum of his attacks and was unconcerned that the Allies would produce a surprise (his view was that his flanks were a responsibility of his superiors). He was clearly disgusted by the loss of 10th Panzer Division to Group Reserve. Nevertheless, conditions were changing and after the comparatively easy charge to the coast, his units met stiffening enemy resistance as they moved north. He referred to the defence of Boulogne in an almost comical fashion, describing how 2nd Panzer Division eventually took the town by getting hold of a ladder to climb the walls of the old town. His farcical account makes the attack sound like a walkover, and underestimates the determination of the defenders and the fierce attacks that 2nd Panzer found it necessary to make, supported by artillery and Luftwaffe bombers. The Division was still cleaning up on the 25th, having spent two days in very tough close-quarter fighting.

Guderian pushed his troops very hard although they were undoubtedly very tired, and even if he found the halt orders irritating, they certainly appreciated the time to rest and restore the condition of their vehicles. Moreover, by committing his divisions to taking well-defended cities like Boulogne and Calais (rather than leaving them to the Luftwaffe), he was getting them tied up in precisely those difficult situations which Hitler had warned about in his secret memo of 9 October 1939, on lessons learnt from the Polish campaign. In this memo, Hitler had stated that the tanks could get lost 'among the maze of endless rows of houses in Belgian towns. It is not necessary for them to attack towns at all.'

Having broken through the French defences on the Meuse, it had taken his Corps just five days (from the 16th to the 20th) to advance from the Meuse bridgehead to Abbeville. However, even in his own understated account, it is quite clear that after the heady rush for the coast, the march north against stiffening resistance was a much more serious affair. Although substantially reinforced by 20th Motorized Infantry and the SS Leibstandarte Adolf Hitler Regiment, 1st Panzer Division took from the 26th until the 29th (when XIX Corps was taken out of the line) to approach the outskirts of Dunkirk. Perversely, Guderian actually stated that: 'the heroic defence of Calais, although worthy of the highest praise, yet had no influence on the development of events outside Dunkirk.' The reality was that his divisions reported heavy fighting and strong resistance at Boulogne, Calais and outside Gravelines. It is therefore debatable how much the 'halt order' on the 24th really prevented Guderian from achieving the stunning victory he claimed. Certainly 1st Panzer was affected as it attacked towards Gravelines, which it started to approach on the 23rd when it came up against 3rd RTR, but his other two divisions were still tied up in their town battles. These troops were not seriously diverted to attack Dunkirk, which may be the reason that Guderian said that the defence of Calais, although it tied up 10th Panzer Division and parts of XIX Corps, did not change events as they developed for the rest of his Corps.

Guderian found it convenient to blame the 'Hitler Halt Order' for the escape of such large numbers of British and French troops from Dunkirk. However, if Guderian had ordered his panzer divisions to occupy and seal off the areas around the major ports instead of pinning them down in classic town battles, he might well have been able to drive his tanks onto the beaches around Dunkirk well before the defence solidified, and the evacuation from Dunkirk might then have been prevented. In the event it was convenient to blame superior officers and Hitler for his delays, rather than his own tactics.

CHAPTER 7

Creation of the Second BEF South of the River Somme

Despite the debacle of Dunkirk, the British leadership had little thought of surrender or dialogue with the Germans. Nevertheless Churchill recognized the dreadful danger of standing alone against the triumphant Germans, and struggled desperately to keep the Anglo-French alliance alive and to keep the French fighting. If France collapsed then there was a very real likelihood of a German invasion of Britain from French ports, aided moreover by the addition of the French Fleet. As the BEF was being evacuated from Dunkirk, hopes of bolstering French resistance fastened on reinforcing the British units discovered to be still fighting in France south of the River Somme.

As already described, the British Support Area south of the Somme had been largely emptied of fighting formations by the move north of the 46th and 23rd Divisions on 18-20 May. However, as the politicians contemplated the total collapse of resistance in the north of France, it was then realized that significant British formations had appeared south of the River Somme and that these could form the basis of continued resistance. These troops, namely the 51st Highland Division, the 1st Armoured Division and the Beauman Division, were of varying quality, but they were still in France, with their equipment, and could provide the basis for future plans. Accordingly, immediately after the Paris Conference of 31 May, Lieutenant General Alan Brooke was appointed to return to France to command these British Forces, which it was hoped would form the nucleus of a new British Expeditionary Force, capable of continuing the struggle.

Three divisions was not much to form the nucleus of an army, but to politicians, desperate for remedies, it could be an evocative token. After all, three divisions was one third of the number of fighting divisions in the BEF, and a plan was quickly developed to double this force with three fresh divisions from England and take up positions alongside the French Army south of the Somme.

This ambitious plan, to reinforce defeat, seems to have ignored the fact that the combined strength of five strong Allied armies comprising more than fifty divisions (the First, Seventh and Ninth French Armies as well as the BEF and the Belgian Army) had just shown they were unable to withstand an attack by only a part of the German Army. And the force left in northern France was not even the equivalent of one third of the original BEF. There were no corps or army troops (with heavy support weapons) to support these divisions and two of them were divisions in but name alone. Only 51st Highland Division had a real artillery complement. In fact, 51st Highland Division was a very strong division, having been reinforced for its detached role on the Maginot Line along the River Saar, south of Luxembourg. Six of its nine infantry battalions consisted of well-trained Territorials from fine Scottish regiments, which could be relied upon to give a good account of themselves, and there were also three regular Scottish battalions. In addition it had six regiments of artillery including one anti-tank regiment, two battalions of machine guns and two battalions of pioneers (quite capable of fighting as infantry), as well as six companies of Royal Engineers. By early June it had suffered significant casualties in the Maginot Line, but the division was still largely intact and numbered some 25,000 men, with much of its support organization, as it was moved from the Saar to take up defensive positions south of the Somme valley.

However, the other two divisions were, as mentioned, divisions in name only. The Beauman Division was an ad hoc collection of men mainly drawn from reinforcement depots in the Rear Area forming some nine infantry battalions, but with no real brigade or divisional organization. As such it was strong in infantry but lacked heavy support weapons such as anti-tank guns and artillery. Brigadier

Beauman was the experienced, energetic officer in charge of the Northern District of the Rear Area, who had commanded a brigade at the end of the First World War. He had done his best to protect his installations with the troops he had been left for local defence, namely the three Lines of Communications battalions: 1/5th Battalion, Sherwood Foresters, 4th Battalion, Border Regiment, and 4th Battalion, The Buffs. There were large stocks of vehicles in his widespread depots so he equipped the 4th Buffs and the 2/6th East Surreys (from 37 Brigade) with new 3-tonne trucks, thereby converting them into a 'flying column' of motorized infantry under Lieutenant Colonel Heselton of the Royal Fusiliers. These four battalions were to become 'A' Brigade of Beauman Division.

In addition Brigadier Beauman began scouring the infantry depots in his area for additional troops who could, at the least, defend some of these valuable stores, and could be formed into infantry, artillery or machine-gun units. Colonel Diggle raised 2,500 rifle-equipped (AMPC) Pioneers from the labour units, which became 'B' Brigade. Colonel Vicary raised five battalion-sized units from the reinforcement depots, initially named after their commanders, namely Perowne, Wait, Ray, Davie, and Meredith, which became 'C' Brigade. Later, another battalion of infantry called Symes's Battalion was raised from the depots. In addition, Beauman had tried to make the best use of troops who found themselves in his area, including utilizing the three battalions of the 46th Division, whose trains had been put out of action on 20 May outside Abbeville. However, the critical weakness was that these were all ad hoc infantry units, which lacked training and particularly artillery, including anti-aircraft and anti-tanks guns.

Nevertheless, to maintain politicians' dreams, a great deal was expected from the third remaining unit, the 1st Armoured Division, which was initially the most powerful fighting formation in the British Army. 1st Armoured Division had been established as a fully equipped armoured formation capable of comparison with German or French armoured divisions and had begun to arrive in France in May, but unfortunately here too, ad hoc changes had already destroyed its capabilities.

Britain had pioneered the concept of using tanks in battle during the First World War. In the 1920s, the British had also pioneered the development of the first experimental armoured division in the world. However, its detractors (among senior generals) had managed to close down the experiment. Heinz Guderian, the German enthusiast for the proper deployment of armour, faced many of the same difficulties from the entrenched views of senior German officers, who still believed the infantry was the 'Queen of the Battlefield'.

However, Guderian gained the support of an influential officer, General Lutz, and then of Adolf Hitler, and by October 1935 he had formed three panzer divisions, each of four tank battalions, together with fully integrated motorized infantry (two battalions) and strong reconnaissance elements. Each division's artillery included twenty-four medium towed guns and twelve towed howitzers, an anti-tank battalion and an anti-aircraft battalion. By the time the attack in the West was launched in May 1940, the Germans were able to field ten armoured divisions (although not all were as well equipped as the best divisions).

The example of what was being achieved by the Germans was at last recognized in Britain and a Mobile Division was created in 1936. Finally, in 1938, it was reborn as an Armoured Division with three elements. The tank components were a Light Brigade of three cavalry regiments (each the equivalent of a battalion) equipped with light tanks, and a Heavy Brigade consisting of three battalions of the Royal Tank Regiment (equipped with heavier tanks, which also mounted a 2-pounder gun). These two brigades were due to be supported by the Division's own Support Group. This consisted of a Royal Horse Artillery (RHA) Regiment (actually using vehicles to tow the guns), a combined Anti-Tank and Anti-Aircraft Regiment, two battalions of infantry carried in armoured vehicles, one Field Company and a Field Park Company, Royal Engineers. (A smaller armoured division (the 7th) under Major General Hobart was also created in Egypt in 1938.)

Based on its formal establishment, 1st Armoured Division was a well-rounded force containing some crack units, although somewhat weak in artillery and in heavy tanks compared to the Germans (as well as the French). However, the Division had been substantially weakened long before its arrival in France in late May 1940. 1st RHA had already been detached and put into GHQ reserve in France in 1939. The Regiment was then attached to the 51st Highland Division when it went forward to the Maginot Line in the Saar valley in April 1940, and never returned to 1st Armoured Division. The two infantry battalions (the Rifle Brigade and KRRC) had been detached for special training in early May and were eventually sent on 23 May to Calais, where together with the Queen Victoria's Rifles and 3rd Royal Tank Regiment (also detached from 1st Armoured Division) they formed 30 Brigade. Under Brigadier Nicholson, this force, supported by some Belgian and French soldiers, held out for three days against the attacks of 1st and 10th Panzer Divisions. In conformity with Churchill's instructions they were not evacuated and fought until overcome.

The effect of these subtractions meant that for most of its time in France, the Support Group really consisted of just the 101st Anti-Tank and Anti-Aircraft Regiment and some Royal Engineers. The 101st had been drawn from two Welsh Territorial gunner units and its four batteries were equipped with two batteries each of twelve mobile Bofors 40mm anti-aircraft guns, and two batteries each of twelve 2-pounder anti-tank guns. However, just before leaving for France, the twenty-four Bofors guns were replaced by ninety-six Lewis machine guns (one could ask the authorities who ordered this change just how effective they expected the men, who had trained on totally different weapons, to be in action against the Luftwaffe). This much-reduced Support Group came ashore in France on 15 May 1940 and proceeded to the training area at Pacy-sur-Eure (35 miles south of Rouen). In the event it never had the chance of exercising or honing its tactics with the rest of the 1st Armoured Division, whose two diminished brigades had been reduced to some 114 light tanks and 143 cruiser tanks.

Some elements of 1st Armoured Division had begun arriving from 15 May, but the main bodies of troops began landing at Cherbourg on the 20th and 22nd. 1st Armoured had been sent to

France with the intention of supporting the BEF, but by the time it had crossed to Cherbourg and assembled it was already too late to join the BEF; it had therefore been placed under French command. Therefore, as the Division began to gather on the training area of Pacy-sur-Eure, it was significantly under establishment and many of its units were still being landed or in transit. At its reduced strength it should have comprised 2nd Armoured Brigade (the Queen's Bays, 9th Queen's Royal Lancers and the 10th Royal Hussars), 3rd Armoured Brigade (2nd and 5th Battalions Royal Tank Regiment) and the remnants of a Support Group.

Barely had Major General Roger Evans begun to assemble his Division on 21 May, when he received conflicting and hopelessly optimistic orders to seize and hold the Somme crossings, with whatever units he had available. This was extremely unfortunate for 1st Armoured Division because GHQ wanted him to deal with 'the mangled remains of six panzer divisions which had come through the Cambrai Peronne gap' and either to protect the flank of the British attack south from Arras (see Chapter 6) or to support the French Seventh Army as it attacked north. As neither of these attacks took place, it was then ordered by General Weygand personally to attack the German positions on the River Somme around Abbeville. Weygand wanted the Germans to be attacked vigorously before they had established proper defensive positions, however, the well-trained German troops had arrived at the Somme area on 21 May and had quickly established very solid anti-tank defences and minefields.

Nevertheless, on 24 May, 2nd Armoured Brigade was ordered to attack across the River Somme, in spite the fact that at that time it only consisted of the Queen's Bays and Brigade Headquarters. However, to support these attacks it was then reinforced by the 4th Border Regiment (from A Brigade of the Beauman Division). Accordingly, a company of the Border Regiment and a troop of the Bays were each ordered to attack at Dreuil, Ailly and Picquigny. Only the attack at Ailly was successful in that two platoons of the Borders actually crossed the River Somme, but the tanks could not cross and, marooned without tank support, the infantry were eventually forced to withdraw. The 4th Borders, a relatively well-trained Territorial unit, which had been in France since October 1939, had thus suffered considerable casualties for no substantive gain. They were the only British unit which was able to fight its way across the River Somme.

The Division was then ordered to attack the Somme crossings in support of Seventh Army on 27 May in the area from St Valery-sur-Somme to Abbeville. It was intended that French artillery and infantry would support the attacks; 2nd Armoured Brigade was ordered to support 2nd DLM (Light Cavalry Division) while 3rd Armoured Brigade was ordered to support 5th DLM. There was no time for careful reconnaissance of the well-established German defences and considerable problems were experienced with artillery co-ordination and infantry support. As a result the attacks against well-placed German anti-tank guns were very costly and the British survivors were forced to retire. The French attacked again on the 28th, with the 9th Lancers in reserve, also without any success, while the remnants of the Bays and 10th Hussars were formed into a Composite Regiment.

On the 29th, General de Gaulle arrived with his 4th Armoured Division and commenced attacks against the German positions around Abbeville. His was one of the strongest remaining French tank formations and he was determined to break through to the River. However, de Gaulle lacked infantry support and asked Major General Fortune and his 51st Highland Division for assistance. Fortune reluctantly agreed to provide some troops.

It had been intended that 51st Highland Division should be grouped with the British 1st Armoured Division, however, by the time it arrived, little remained of the strength of 1st Armoured Division other than a Composite Regiment and a combined anti-tank and anti-aircraft regiment. Therefore Major General Fortune did his best to help de Gaulle, an assistance which de Gaulle said he fondly remembered throughout his time in London as leader of the Free French. However, the Germans were in strong defensive positions and despite valiant efforts little real progress was made. After several days of fruitless attacks de Gaulle was forced to withdraw. Then on 4 June, Fortune was ordered to carry out fresh attacks on the Abbeville bridgehead, for which operation the newly arrived French

31st (Alpine) Division was placed under his command. In addition there were some 160 French tanks from the two light cavalry divisions as well as a considerable reinforcement of French artillery. The attack, however, was not a success, mainly owing to the difficulty of arranging effective co-operation between British and French infantry, guns and tanks at such short notice, and the 51st Division again suffered fairly heavy casualties, for no gain.

On 5 June, the Germans finally attacked with overwhelming force all along the so-called thinly held Weygand Line. The French had scraped together almost fifty divisions to man the line, but many were under strength and they were hopelessly outnumbered by the Germans, who had made good their losses and were able to attack with 137 fresh divisions. The area from the coast around Abbeville to Amiens was held by the French Tenth Army with two corps. The left-hand corps, the French IXth Corps, in addition to the Highlanders, consisted of four French divisions: the weakened 2nd and 5th Light Cavalry Divisions, as well as the 31st and 40th Infantry Divisions.

CHAPTER 8

51st Highland Division on the Saar and on the Somme

The 51st Highland Division had established one of the most distinguished fighting records among the British divisions of the BEF in the First World War. As a Territorial division it had provided reinforcements to other serving divisions in France until it went out to the Western Front early in 1915. It took part in the Third Battle of Ypres in July 1916 and distinguished itself in its famous action on 13 November 1916, when it took the heavily fortified village of Beaumont-Hamel and established its reputation as one of the fiercest assault divisions in the BEF. In April 1917, it made a significant advance of 10,000 yards in the Battle of Arras, alongside the Canadians (who captured Vimy Ridge). It also achieved a significant advance at Cambrai in November 1917 and was one of the four divisions lent to the French to support the French Fifth and Tenth Armies in the Battle of Tardenois in July 1918. It then raced back to join the British attacks of August 1918 which broke the German defences in front of the Hindenburg Line, and led to the wholesale retreat of the German Army. Finally, it took part in the rapid advance of the BEF in October 1918, which led to the Germans requesting an armistice. Some of its units stayed in Europe to provide part of the occupation forces in Germany, but the rest were demobilized. The Division suffered huge casualties, earning a ferocious reputation and being described by the Germans as one of the most feared assault units in the British Army.

Most infantry soldiers owed their loyalty to their own regiment, and deservedly many individual regiments had achieved recognition for their valour. However, the identity of the kilt-wearing 51st

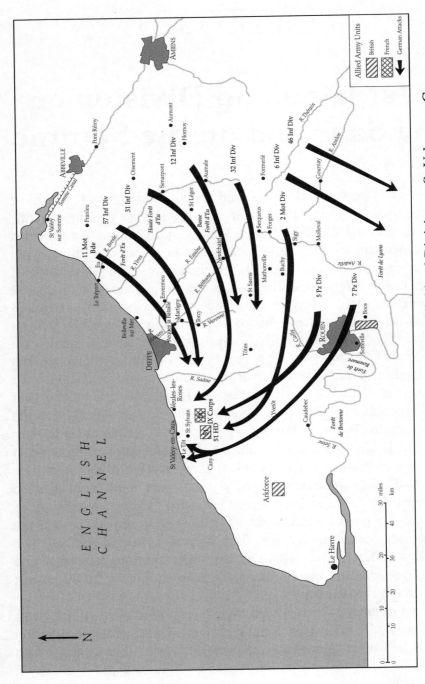

Map 4. Encirclement of IX Corps and 51st Highland Division at St Valery-en-Caux.

Highland Division as a division had subsumed that of its individual units and it had become a legendary name by the time it was returned to the UK in 1919. Therefore, when the division was mobilized again in 1939, the individual regiments, as well as the units of the supporting arms, once again took pride in their membership of the Highland Division. The Division was initially organized with three brigades each of three battalions of Territorial infantry battalions drawn from five proud Scottish regiments: The Black Watch, The Seaforth Highlanders, The Queen's Own Cameron Highlanders, The Gordon Highlanders, and The Argyle and Sutherland Highlanders.

The Division landed in a frozen France at Le Havre at the end of January 1940. Instead of joining the strength of the three corps (comprising nine divisions) of the BEF on the Belgian frontier, it first relieved the French 21st Division near Armentières. Then, as a further concrete expression of solidarity with the French during the so-called 'Phoney War', it was decided to put the Division directly into the Maginot Line where it was expected to gain valuable experience. This was a repetition of the loan of the earlier division to the French in the Champagne battles of 1918, which had so decisively achieved the victory of the Second Battle of the Marne. Accordingly, in late April 1940, 51st Highland Division was sent to the Maginot Line to relieve a French division.

Service in the Maginot Line was seen as an important and testing role for a newly arrived division, and to strengthen its level of experience it was reorganized with three Regular Army battalions replacing three Territorial battalions, so that each brigade then had one Regular battalion as well as two Territorial battalions. As well as its three brigades of infantry, 51st Highland Division had three regiments of field artillery (17th, 23rd and 75th) and the 51st Anti-Tank Regiment RA. It was decided, perhaps partially to impress the French, but also to strengthen its defensive capability, that the Division would be given additional support troops (mostly from III Corps). These included a light armoured reconnaissance regiment (1st Lothians and Border Yeomanry) and two extra artillery regiments: 1st RHA (less one battery, which was replaced by a battery from 97th Field Regiment) and 51st Medium Regiment (with two batteries of heavy howitzers). Its defensive capability was further enhanced with two machine-gun battalions (7th Battalion, Royal Northumberland Fusiliers and 1st Battalion, Princess Louise's Kensington Regiment) and two pioneer battalions (7th Battalion, Royal Norfolk Regiment and 6th Battalion, Royal Scots Fusiliers), as well as the 213th Army Field Company Royal Engineers. This was a considerable enhancement and as a result 51st Highland Division, with six regiments of artillery, two machine-gun battalions and five companies of engineers was virtually a mini-corps (indeed it had most of the support troops from III Corps). It also substantially increased its tail of transport, ordinance, maintenance and medical units, not to mention the Royal Signals who ensured the communications of a division of some 25,000 men. When on the move, the Division's columns, comprising some 3,000 vehicles, would consume an average of 16,000 gallons of petrol per day.

By 1 May, the Division was placed under command of the French Third Army in the Metz Fortified Region, as one of the three covering divisions in the Fortified Sector of Thionville. 51st Highland Division was given a critical role in the defence of the Maginot Line positions east of Hombourg-Budange (which lies about 20 kilometres east of Thionville) close to the Saar River and the German Siegfried Line. In the rear of the Division lay the great underground fortress of Hackenberg, which was built into the hillside overlooking the small village of Veckring.

Hackenberg was claimed to be the largest of all the Maginot forts with seventeen battle blocks and two entrance blocks connected by over 10 kilometres of tunnels. Its garrison from the 164th RIF (Fortress Infantry Regiment) and the 153rd RAP (Garrison Artillery Regiment) comprised some forty-two officers and 1,040 men. They manned a series of observation and firing positions in three main positions equipped mainly with 135mm mortars and 75mm gun howitzers, and automatic machine guns firing from retractable armoured turrets and embrasures. Hackenberg was one of the most important forts covering the eastern approaches to Metz and the first to be fully completed. It had been built and equipped between the years 1930 and 1935 by some 1,800 workers.

Hackenberg was so impressive that it was regularly promoted as an example of the impregnability of the Maginot Line. In a highly publicised event on 9 December 1939, Hackenberg was visited by King George VI, accompanied by Lord Gort, the Duke of Gloucester and General Gamelin. In early 1940 there was a much quieter visit by Winston Churchill. Hackenberg had many of the characteristics of a concrete ship built into the hills guarding the French eastern frontier. It contained its own small hospital, kitchens and recreation areas for the troops forced to live in the fort, although the troops were usually accommodated in barracks in the local village of Veckring. Like virtually all of the Maginot forts, it could not be subdued by the Germans despite the thinning out of its interval troops and garrisons, and remained in French hands until some days after the armistice of 25 June. Hackenberg itself was considered almost impregnable and was not directly assaulted by the Germans (although the Luftwaffe had repeatedly bombed it, with an equal lack of success). It opened fire and duelled with enemy artillery from 15 May as the covering troops fell back, and although completely surrounded by enemy formations it displayed its capacity to resist attack by opening fire on 22 June to protect the nearby fortress of Michelsberg.

After the armistice on 25 June, negotiations were commenced to surrender the forts, which was finally done on 4 July; a technical detachment was left behind to show the Germans how to operate the fort. After their victory in 1940, the Germans once again incorporated Alsace and Lorraine into the German Reich and forcibly conscripted the local population into the German Army, although they never attempted to make use of the Maginot forts as such and allowed many of them to fall into disrepair. Later they also stripped many of the weapons and fittings from the Maginot forts for use in the Atlantic Wall, and for a while Hackenberg was used as an underground factory by the German company, Klockner Humbold Deutz. In November 1944, Hackenberg was actually attacked from the west, when a 'stay behind' party of Germans in Bastion 8, armed with three 75mm guns, attempted to hold up the American Third Army (commanded by General Patton) in its approach to the Siegfried Line. The US 90th Infantry Division brought up some M12

155mm SP guns (originally of French design and manufacture from 1918), which eventually subdued the Germans. The resulting damage to Bastion 8 was partially repaired, but can still be seen clearly today.

Despite that damage, Hackenberg is still one of the best-preserved installations in the Maginot Line, with its power plant, railway and many lifts still working. It is also an extremely interesting working museum and is regularly open to visitors. The entrance to the fortress can be found just to the south of the village of Veckring, where there is also to be found a very small memorial to the 51st Highland Division. Conducted tours (which take about two hours) are led by enthusiastic local supporters and are very worthwhile. For an above-ground impression of the vastness of this fortress it is worth following the small road up to the right of the entrance, which leads to the old German chapel on the top of the ridge (at 347 metres above sea level). On the way you will pass other sealed battle blocks and there are extensive views towards Germany as well as a view of the observation cupolas which sit close to the chapel.

Having taken over its exposed positions close to the border, 51st Highland Division was soon actively engaged in patrolling and defending against the Germans in the Ligne de Contact (Line of Contact), some 10 miles in advance of the main line of Maginot forts, even before the main attacks began on 10 May. The Division held a sector about 5 miles wide facing almost due east towards the German border. Its front line of defensive positions connected woods and villages from Heydewald in the north, along the eastern side of the Grossenwald to le Harbuch, through Colmen and on to Tiergarten Wood.

51st Highland Division was sandwiched between the French 2nd Division on its left and the French 42nd Division on its right. The divisional area was divided into three brigade sectors: 153 Brigade on the left with advanced positions around Remeling; 154 Brigade in the middle around Grindorff; and 152 Brigade covering the right flank around Colmen. Each brigade had one battalion forward in the Ligne de Contact (Contact Line) and the Ligne de Soutien (Support Line) just behind it. A second battalion held the Ligne de Recueil (Line of Consolidation) (about halfway between the Maginot forts and the Contact Line) and the third battalion was held in reserve, ready to man the intervals between the forts. Also well concealed behind the forward infantry defences were the artillery and machine-gun positions. The battalions of each brigade relieved each other in the Contact Line on a regular basis.

The Contact Line was a series of defensive positions located about 3 miles (5 kilometres) or less from the German border. Immediately after taking up their posts the battalions, assisted by their engineers and pioneers, began improving the positions by replacing some of the French mini-forts of logs with sandbagged and revetted fire-trench positions surrounded by thick barbed-wire entanglements. All the French villages close to the border had been evacuated since September 1939 and were eerily silent to the Scots, who occupied their trenches in the woods overlooking them. Each night the battalions also followed a policy of aggressive patrolling of the woods, which contained parties of equally aggressive observing or patrolling Germans. Tiergarten Wood on the right was less than a mile from where the German border bent west and was frequently the scene of conflicts with German listening patrols.

Today (almost seventy years later) it is still possible to see evidence of some of the Scottish defences which have remained almost untouched in the woods of Heydewald, le Wölscher and Grossenwald, especially overlooking the small hamlet of Betting, which was deserted in 1940 and occupied by a forward section of Scots. The forward trenches and company positions, as well as the bullet-marked trees, can even now be seen quite clearly in the trees above Betting. A visit to this evocative area can easily be combined with a tour of the great hidden fortress of Hackenberg at Veckring.

After 12 May, the German infantry attacks supported by heavy artillery barrages began in earnest, but were held in the forward positions. The Germans attempted to tap the telephone wires which ran from the platoon back to the company positions, but were foiled by the Scots' use of Gaelic. On the morning of 14 May very heavy shelling began and it was reported that on one company front of the 5th Gordons, the Germans had fired 3,600 shells within one and a half hours. D Company of the 5th Gordons, holding Heydewald on the far left of the 51st Highland Division sector, was hit by repeated box barrages, which prevented the forward posts from being supported and accordingly these were eventually overcome and captured. D Company was eventually forced to withdraw with just twenty-eight survivors, having suffered seventy casualties. Eventually, by the 16th, Major General Fortune decided to withdraw to the ridge of the Kalenhofen Forest, but was then forced to retire to the Ligne de Recueil (Consolidation Line) in order to conform to the French divisions on both flanks which had also been pressed very hard. Although the defences of the Ligne de Recueil were incomplete, the Division carried out demolitions and improved obstacles to slow the German advance, and continued patrolling to inflict casualties. The Germans, for their part, were content to keep large numbers of Maginot defenders tied down – while the decisive battle was won in the north – and avoided pressing into the killing grounds in front of the Maginot forts.

The Division had sustained casualties but was undaunted when, on 20 May, it completed its tour, being ordered into reserve to cover Paris, and was replaced by a French division. At that stage, although the Germans had already broken through on the Meuse, the French Army was still relatively well organized and following its normal replacement procedures. However, over the next few days this organization fell apart as the Germans poured west along the north bank of the Somme to split and surround the French armies, and the BEF between the Somme and the Channel coast. At first the Division concentrated on Varennes, but the orders were frequently changed and eventually it was ordered to move to Normandy. By a mixture of road and rail parties it finally arrived in the area of the River Bresle, between le Tréport and Blangy on 28 May. 51st Highland Division was once again in the territory allotted to the British for their lines of communication (the Northern Sector commanded by the Brigadier Beauman) and was able to be resupplied.

At first it was intended that 51st Highland Division and 1st Armoured Division would be combined to form a small British corps. However, 1st Armoured Division was already so worn down by the futile attack orders that it had been given that all that remained in the area was a Composite Regiment and its so-called Support Group. 51st Highland Division was therefore placed together with the French 31st and 40th Infantry Divisions, and the French 2nd and 5th DLM (Light Cavalry Divisions), under command of General Ihler, commanding the French IX Corps (half of the French Tenth Army). It moved into the coastal area and was allocated quite a wide front of some 20 miles south of the River Somme from Senarpont to Eu on the coast.

CHAPTER 9

Churchill and the Brittany Redoubt

Following the German attack on 10 May, events moved so swiftly that formal inter-governmental conferences of the same kind as had been held between the Allies, normally in Paris, could no longer be convened. Travel to France became extremely dangerous as the Luftwaffe gained control of the skies and the numerous aircraft of the French Air Force disappeared into the interior of France or to North Africa. According to Len Deighton's calculations, the French, after their armistice, still had available in their territory over 6,000 aircraft of which at least 2,000 were suitable for front-line use. Despite this growing danger, Churchill, with almost complete disregard for his safety, made five visits to France during May and June, to meet with and support the French, particularly Prime Minister Reynaud, and try to keep the French fighting.

On Tuesday, 11 June, Winston Churchill set off for his fifth and final visit to France accompanied by Anthony Eden, General Dill, General Ismay, Brigadier Lund, Captain Berkeley (Ismay's assistant and translator) and Major General Spears. Their aircraft, the special Flamingo, was escorted by twelve Hurricane fighters. The French Government had moved from Paris and the meeting was arranged to take place at Weygand's chateau at Briare, south-east of Orleans in the Loire Valley. The French were represented by Prime Minister Reynaud, Marshal Pétain, General de Gaulle (recently appointed Under-Secretary for National Defence), de Margerie (Reynaud's Chef de Cabinet) and the Air Force General, de Vuillemin. Their aircraft landed on the aerodrome at Briare, which looked particularly bleak and deserted, and it took some time before some cars eventually arrived to pick up the British party. The British did not feel really welcome (like unwelcome poor relations at a family funeral, according to Spears), as most of the French (apart from de Gaulle) seemed overcome by the military disaster they were facing. Churchill and the other British, on the other hand, affected great confidence. When the conference began at 1900 hrs, Reynaud began by discussing the projected air raids planned for that evening by Anglo-French air forces against Italian targets in Genoa, Turin and Milan. The French wanted to stop the operations because they felt that their own cities of Marseilles and Lyons were completely unprotected and vulnerable to Italian retaliation. Churchill was delighted to inform them that the operations could not be stopped as the aircraft had already left Britain. (In the event the French attempted to block the airfield at Salon near Marseilles, where the aircraft from RAF Bomber Command (Haddock Force) were to land for refuelling and then take off for Italy.)

Churchill then said that the purpose of the conference was to discuss how the British and French should take the War forward, despite the current difficult situation. Churchill went on to stress that Britain would continue to fight the Germans no matter what. He anticipated that the Germans might stabilize their front in France and turn on England, which he would welcome as it would take the pressure off the French and allow the Royal Air Force to destroy the Luftwaffe. Churchill did his best to talk up the positives and the continuing efforts to increase the current British capability, stressing that a British infantry division was deployed around Le Mans, and that a Canadian division with seventy-two guns was landing that night. This meant that Britain would have four divisions already in France, with another division due around 20 June. He proffered the prospect that if only the French could hold out, then by the spring of 1941, Britain would have twenty to twenty-five divisions to place at the disposal of the French High Command.

Spears said he detected the barely suppressed irritation of the French at the inadequacy of this reinforcement. Weygand then commented on the current military situation, which was bleak: in every sector the troops were exhausted and outnumbered; he could do nothing to restore the situation anywhere because he had no more reserves. He attempted to mollify his extremely negative outlook by referring to the French divisions which had been evacuated from Dunkirk and were now being reconstituted in Normandy, and that perhaps, together with the troops coming back from Narvik, and the new British divisions, there might be a chance to do something. However, there was no guarantee that his exhausted troops could hang on for much longer. The meeting was then joined by General Georges, who painted a very similar picture. He estimated that at least thirty-five divisions out of the original 105 Allied divisions had been lost as well as the mechanized cavalry and most of the armoured divisions. Moreover, having lost the very best divisions, at least twenty-five of those divisions still fighting were completely dislocated. They were opposed by Germans who outnumbered them three to one, and added to this problem was the fact that Italy had declared war on France a day earlier.

Churchill attempted to counter this dismal prospect by pointing out that the Allies had faced and overcome immense difficulties in the past, particularly against the powerful German spring offensives of 1918. General Dill, taking the lead from Churchill and attempting to placate the French, said that Weygand could use the troops now in France as he thought fit and not even wait for full divisions to be formed. This reckless offer was immediately taken up by Weygand (it eventually almost led to the loss of part of the 52nd Division). Churchill again went on to suggest that the French could absorb huge numbers of the enemy if they fought in Paris. As Weygand had that day ordered that Paris be declared an 'open city', this caused the French to freeze. Unmindful of this, Churchill went on to say that although Britain would continue to support France with aircraft, they were unable to throw their last aircraft into the battle as there was a bigger battle coming up, namely the 'Battle of Britain'.

Churchill was limited in what he could offer. He had already held a meeting of the Cabinet before coming to France at which it had been decided that, no matter what, twenty-five fighter squadrons had to be kept back for the defence of Britain. This was clearly disappointing for the French who thought that only massive injections of air power could save them, and they continued to argue for some time that only additional air resources, based in France, could change the outcome of the War. But the British held firm, resolved not to risk their last reserves of air power, and Churchill again brought up the subject of bridgeheads on the Atlantic, which meant principally Brittany. Weygand said the idea was still being studied by General Altmayer, but given that he was not in favour of this idea, it did not receive solid backing from anyone except Churchill and de Gaulle. Unfortunately, Weygand had no other ideas for improving the situation, nor for that matter had General Georges. Guerrilla warfare, Churchill's other hobby horse, held no promise of being able to hold up the Germans, and it was becoming clear that the anti-war party, including Pétain, were just waiting to be able to arrange an armistice with the Germans.

The conference resumed next morning, but the strategic reality could not be changed. Churchill reconfirmed his promises of maintaining the air support of Air Marshal Barrett's Advanced Air Striking Force (AASF) as well as six to eight squadrons of fighters being sent over France every day. He also suggested that perhaps a counter-attack by ten divisions in the Lower Seine area, and the determined holding of Paris, would absorb the Germans. All of these ideas were met with unbelieving silence by the French. While Weygand had no intention of defending Paris having already declared it an open city, Pétain, Reynaud, Weygand and Georges could not imagine that anything other than a huge commitment of air power by the British could save their exhausted troops (remarkably no mention was made of the huge French Air Force, which, having been startled from its forward air bases, was largely intact, but hardly to be seen).

Churchill later admitted that he was also constrained in his arguments by the knowledge that Britain had done so comparatively little (despite its population of 48 million) to support the campaign in France, and most of the suffering had hitherto fallen on the French people. It is clear that he and Reynaud agreed to try to draw a defensive line across the foot of the Brittany peninsula. In his memoirs Churchill asserts that it was a sound plan, and that although difficult, even a few weeks resistance would have maintained contact with Britain and enabled large troop withdrawals to North Africa. Protected by the large, modern French Navy and with the support of the British Mediterranean Fleet, the French Government could have continued the struggle against the Germans, who would have found it very difficult to deal with a resistant French. The only alternative was surrender and it was significant that Marshal Pétain was already in favour of seeking an armistice. Before leaving, Churchill received a personal commitment from Admiral Darlan that the French Fleet would never be allowed to fall into the hands of the Germans.

Returning unescorted from Briare, the sombre British party flew in the Flamingo over Le Havre where smoke from burning installations filled the sky. The British were caught in a terrible dilemma. While France was clearly on the edge of total collapse, perhaps the Germans were equally worn out, although there was little evidence of this. If the British failed to provide real help then France would collapse and Britain would be left alone to fight an enlarged and victorious Germany, and could even be invaded within weeks. On the other hand, no help could be provided to France without desperately weakening the ability of Britain to continue to defend itself against Germany. Churchill had already committed the only two fully formed divisions in Britain (the 52nd and the 1st Canadian) to go to France, and had promised to send the refitting 3rd Division by the end of the month. This left the cupboard in Britain totally bare. How could Britain possibly defeat a sudden invasion with no trained and organized troops, not to mention virtually no artillery and no tanks? As they returned to London that evening came the bombshell of the news of the surrender of the 51st Highland Division at St Valery-en-Caux that morning.

The surrender of such a famous division, and moreover one which had been increased in size to almost a small corps, was a bitter blow. The 51st Highland Division was to have been the strong nucleus around which the Second BEF was to be built. The surrender of such an important division was not only a portent of what could have happened to the whole BEF, but also a forewarning of what might happen if the reinforcements being sent to France were abandoned by the French, or lost in hopeless last-ditch stands. Even while the French were requesting more bombers and fighters to be stationed in France, the refusal of the French to allow Marshal Barratt's heavy bombers to take off from Salon, and other airfields near Marseilles, was another bitter example of the dangers of leaving hostages to fortune in France. However, Churchill was still determined to provide support for the French and keep them in the war.

Churchill was a warrior politician. His education had been as cavalry officer, and he had had many adventures in South Africa. In the First World War, after losing office as a result of the Gallipoli failure, he had requested command of a Scottish battalion in the trenches in France. His initial reaction to the 'Miracle of Dunkirk' was to turn it to a positive advantage by mounting a counter-offensive against the Germans. He thought in terms of landing (or threatening to land) on any part of the European coast held by the Germans. To this end he gave instructions on 4 June that raiding forces should be formed and trained. This order eventually led to the formation of the Commandos and the build-up of an amphibious landing capability, but this initiative was to take some years before it provided significant results. Meanwhile, it was in conformity with this aggressive stance that Churchill wanted to use the troops left in France to stay engaged with the Germans and demonstrate a commitment to the French.

On 12 June, as Churchill's aircraft lifted off from Briare, he was certain that the three British divisions already in France would soon be joined by three others, newly landed from Britain. In Normandy and Brittany, they would be able to join the eight divisions of the Tenth Army and be reinforced by many other French units, as well as the troops which had been landed at Cherbourg from Dunkirk. It was not much but it might be enough to convince the French that Britain was providing real support and would provide tangible proof that the British could support a toehold of resistance in the north of France. Even so, it was equally clear that the French Army, with a front-line strength reduced to less than fifty divisions, could not hope to sustain a viable defence for long against fresh German attacks by more than 130 divisions all along the width of France.

). A Scottish Piper and soldier in front of one of the armoured emergency exit doors from the
piece Maginot Line fortress of Fort Hackenberg, which was never subdued.

highly publicized visit in December 1939, King George VI inspects the impressive facilities
rmaments of the recently completed Fort Hackenberg.

3. 51st Highland Division firing and observation trenches in the woods in the Line of Contact.

4. The trenches and positions excavated the 51st Highland Division are still vis almost seventy year later in the woods a Betting.

5. View today overlooking the small village of Betting which was deserted in 1940 and used as the forward position of the 51st Highland Division.

rance to Fort Hackenberg today. Volunteers conduct visitors to view the working gun
rms, kitchens, hospital, several museums and the great diesel engines, which provide power
entilation.

great ruined fortress of Arques-la-Bataille. Some of the units camped near here were grouped
rkforce, which went ahead to establish a defensive line at Fécamp and were evacuated to
nd.

8. View of the harbour of
St Valery-en-Caux at high
water today.

9. St Valery-en-Caux. Maison Henri IV.
One of the few ancient buildings of the
town centre fortunate not to be
destroyed by Rommel's artillery, it is
now the town museum.

ew of the narrow tidal channel of St Valery-en-Caux, overlooked by the cliffs which were
ied by German tanks and artillery, which prevented the evacuation of 40,000 Allied troops.

ew of the steep 40-metre chalk cliffs from Veules-les-Roses. By mid-1944 Rommel had ensured
hese cliffs were laced with carefully sited gun positions to deter invasion.

12. 12 June 1940. Major General Rommel, sporting his new Knight's Cross over his Pour le Méri poses at the surrender of IX Corps close to a disgusted looking Major General Fortune.

13. Rommel takes the surrender of senior French generals on the quay at St Valery-en-Caux.

14. Advancing German troops pass columns of Allied prisoners.

15. A German soldier searches French prisoners.

16 (*Left*). 8 April 1940. The *Admiral Hipper* sinking the *Gloworm*. Although heavily outgunned, sh attempted to ram the *Hipper* and caused a 40-foot gash before she sank.

17 (*Right*). 30 May 1940. German artillery and mines sink the French destroyer *Bourrasque*, crow with French troops, near Dunkirk.

18. *La Patrie*, a French warship crowded with evacuated soldiers from Veules-les-Roses.

June 1940. HMT *Lancastria* is continually bombed by German aircraft until a Ju88 finally hits it
...g it to capsize and sink with the loss of thousands of men outside St Nazaire.

...une 1942. Survivors
...n the sinking of the
Laconia standing on
...erman U-boat *U156*
...re they were forced
...back into the shark-
infested sea.

21. View of the beautiful
village of Veules-les-
Roses today. The fishing
village grew up
alongside the small
rivers which flow out
through the break in the
high chalk cliffs, which
are such a defining
feature of this coast.

22. View of dispirited British and French prisoners who had defended the area, beginning their captivity against a similar background in Veules-les-Roses.

23. Soldiers of the 51st Highland Division manning a tank barrier against the onslought from five German divisions.

ottish warrant officer accounts for survivors while watched by a German captor.

me troops got away by scrambling down the 40-metre cliffs using makeshift ropes.

26. British prisoners beginning their long march into captivity in Germany.

27. Allied soldiers who did not get away being marshalled by Germans (some 3,321 did get awa
ships from Veules-les-Roses).

28. A German machine gunner takes aim on the *Cérons*. It had had taken some 300 men on board before grounding – the men were transferred to another ship.

29. The wreck of the French patrol ship P21, *Cérons*, showing three of its four main 100mm cannon pointing to the sky. It was sunk 12 June 1940 trying to rescue soldiers from the beach.

30. Two of the guns were eventually rescued from the wreck of the *Cérons*. On the initiative of the Mayor, M. Claire, they are now displayed on the hill overlooking Veules-les-Roses as a permanent memorial.

31. 18 June 1940. The French destroy two of their submarines in the construction yards at Cherbourg.

August 1944. Scottish troops advance through the bocage, led by a piper.

September 1944. Liberation Day. Pipes and drums playing in Veules-les-Roses. 51st Highland
ion liberates St Valery-en-Caux and Veules-les-Roses. The German garrison had pulled back to
vre, which soon fell to the 51st Highland Division.

34. June 1944. Germa[n] troops experience the disappointment of trudging into captivit[y]

35. Military cemetery of St Valery-en-Caux where many of the 51st Highland Division still lie. There are 234 Commonwealth headstones and 218 French in this peaceful cemetery.

36. On the cliffs overlooking St Valery[-en-]Caux, surrounded by [the] debris of futile Germa[n] defences, stands the granite memorial to t[he] 51st Highland Divisio[n]

Meanwhile, as the party landed, they were met with the terrible news that the 51st Highland Division had not been evacuated from St Valery-en-Caux, but had been forced to surrender. Churchill was deeply affected by the loss of the 51st Highland Division, realizing only too well that the Division could have been saved if the French had sent it to Rennes or Le Havre before it had been cut off. However, his crocodile tears over its loss because of the failures of the French (effectively Weygand) were not really accurate. He wrote in his own history that it had been obvious three days earlier that the 51st were in danger. Actually he was not to know that it was partly Major General Fortune's own decision to stay with the slow-moving French 31st Division which exposed him to the encirclement by Rommel's fast-moving panzers. Fortune was not the sort of man who would abandon allies who had fought bravely alongside his Division, just because their horses could go no faster. Moreover, a different solution had been available to the British. Lieutenant General Brooke had already been appointed commander of the new II Corps, which would also include any British troops still in France, and he could have ordered a more rapid withdrawal of the 51st Highland Division. However, despite being appointed on 2 June, he did not actually appear in France until the 13th, when he formally assumed command of all British troops and, after a perfunctory meeting, sent the former interim GOC, Lieutenant General Sir Henry Karslake back to the UK. By then it was already too late. Even as Brooke finally embarked for France, 51st Highland Division was being forced to surrender to Rommel's troops.

Once actually in France, Brooke's sole aim seems to have been to get British troops out as fast as possible. Although he signed up to the plan for the establishment of a defensive line in the Rennes area with Generals Weygand and Georges on the morning of 14 June, he seems to have spent the rest of the day ensuring that the plan was not implemented. Not for the last time Brooke was destined to act to restrain the 'romantic' ambitions of the Prime Minister.

Was Brooke the wrong man to have sent to France? He certainly did not hasten to get there. When ordered by Churchill to continue supporting the French he argued for immediate evacuation of all

THE BRITISH ARMY IN FRANCE AFTER DUNKIRK

British troops. Even though the 51st had been lost, there were still enough effective elements and stores to constitute four or five divisions, which could have been used for the defence of Brittany, and these could have been reinforced by the French Tenth Army which was also retiring into Brittany. It was therefore possible that a reasonable defence could have been put together over the following weeks and it would have been strengthened by the 3rd Division after 22 June. There is no doubt that much more could have been done to put together a credible defence by an energetic commander and therefore the British would not have been seen as running out so precipitately on the French. As a result the French resistance might have gone on for much longer and the Germans would not have had such an obvious walkover victory.

However, it has to be admitted that even these best efforts would only have postponed the inevitable. In the long run it would have been as pointless as continuing the battle at Narvik, where the Allies were successfully driving the remnants of the small German garrison into Sweden, while the rest of Norway was being ruthlessly occupied by German troops. Or, perhaps as significant for the outcome of the War, was the way in which the French Army of the Alps successfully held up a far larger invading Italian force, until the signing of the armistice brought an end to their resistance.

Within even a few weeks, the Germans would have been able to turn and use an Army Group to reduce the Breton Redoubt. Moreover, given their overwhelming air power based on local airfields, there would have been no Breton Dunkirk. Instead there would probably have been a series of repeat 'St Valery's' at bases around Brest, Cherbourg and St Nazaire, as isolated bodies of troops were forced to lay down their arms. At the very least this would have resulted in the surrender of at least four more divisions and base personnel, and probably the loss of many thousands of men by drowning at sea. It would necessarily have led to the further significant losses by the Royal Navy and the Royal Air Force as they attempted to support or evacuate the British troops in Brittany. As such this almost certainly would have so weakened the Army, Navy and Air Force that the Battle of Britain could not have been won, and a weakened and overstretched Royal Navy might not have been able to stop serious amphibious landings and resupply on the British coast. Indeed, if the Germans had chosen to make their attack on Britain before reducing the Breton Redoubt (which they clearly had the resources to attempt) then victory would have been even more certain. If such an invasion had been launched in late June or July of 1940, the British Army would have been so disorganized and weakened, as well as lacking tanks and artillery, that it would not have been able to defeat a serious German invasion.

The Brittany Redoubt was never tested, but could it have led to a different outcome to the War? In the end the decision to pursue this possibility came down to a struggle between two men, Churchill and Brooke – a struggle between a political visionary and a realistic soldier.

CHAPTER 10

51st Highland Division in Normandy and salvation of Arkforce

At first 51st Highland Division took up positions behind the French 4th Armoured Division and assisted General de Gaulle in the attacks which he made on the Somme crossings, which were stoutly defended by the Germans. After de Gaulle left, 51st Highland Division was ordered to begin another attack on 4 June to regain the Somme crossings, with the French 31st Alpine Division and 2nd DLM under command. However, there was little time for reconnaissance or proper planning co-ordination of the substantial artillery assets in attacking the positions, which the Germans had had two weeks to fortify. Not surprisingly the attacks all failed.

The following day, at four o clock in the morning, the Germans attacked in strength all along the so-called Weygand Line. Nine German Armies comprising 137 divisions began a heavy artillery and bombing attack against less than fifty French divisions strung out along the Somme and Aisne valleys. The French had wisely constructed fortified hedgehogs supported by their excellent artillery and defended themselves stoutly, but given the overwhelming German superiority, could only hold out for one or two days. 51st Highland Division and 31st Division, already exhausted by their attacks the day before, had a total front of almost 40 miles to defend against the pressure from the German Fourth Army. Fourth Army comprised Hoth's Corps with 5th and 7th Panzer Divisions, as well as a Motorized Division, 11th Motorized Brigade and 1st Cavalry Division, and six infantry divisions.

All three of the Scottish brigades were placed forward: 154 Brigade on the left south of St Valery-sur-Somme, 153 Brigade in the centre, and 152 Brigade on the right occupying the area south of Abbeville. However, under the tremendous pressure from the Germans, supported by artillery, mortars and Stukas, the Division was forced to give ground as it suffered heavy casualties. The pressure was heaviest on the left where the German 11th Motorized Brigade and the 57th and 12th Infantry Divisions were attacking. Only the rapid firing of the divisional artillery prevented the Germans from overrunning the Division. The 7th Argyll and Sutherland Highlanders, defending the village of Franleu, had twenty-three officers and almost 500 men as casualties, and 154 Brigade was reduced to half strength.

By the following morning, 7 June, the Division was joined by 'A' Brigade of Beauman's Division (consisting of 4th Buffs, 4th Border Regiment and 5th Sherwood Foresters, comprising some 900 men) as it attempted to hold a line along the Bresle River from Eu to Senarpont, with the Composite Regiment, the 2/6th East Surreys and the Lothians and Border Horse defending the open flank along the Andelle River.

General Ihler and IX Corps were under orders from General Weygand to continue to hold the Bresle River line 'at all costs'. Hoth's XV Panzer Corps, with the 5th and 7th Panzer Divisions, waited for the infantry to clear the way through the main French defences before forcing their way through the Weygand Line and heading for Rouen, thereby splitting the French Tenth Army in two. The Bresle defenders, supported by their strong artillery, were holding out against the frontal attacks but were being outflanked. In spite of it becoming quite clear in London that the British and French units of IX Corps were in danger of being encircled in the Havre peninsula unless they were withdrawn south across the Seine, all representations to Weygand failed to change his orders to defend the Bresle line.

Hoth's tanks then sliced through the British defenders guarding the flank of 51st Highland Division between Aumale and Forges-les-Eaux. On the 8th, Rommel planned to advance on Rouen and stage a threat to the town, but then by a 'coup de main' he hoped to take the bridge across the Seine at Elbouf, thereby outflanking a major part of the French defenders. However, the River Andelle at Signy was defended by B and C Brigades of Beauman's Division (including many Royal Engineers) and they blew the bridge just in time to slow his advance significantly. The British defenders suffered grievously as they conducted a fighting withdrawal until nightfall, by which time they had also run out of ammunition.

By 8 June, 51st Highland Division and 31st Alpine Division were still on the Bresle, while 'B' and 'C' Brigades of Beauman's Division occupied a secondary defence line along the Bethune and Andelle rivers between the Seine and Dieppe. Under command of Beauman's Division (but with very limited control) a further defence line around Rouen had been established with Symes's Battalion (with four 2-pounder guns) defending Isneauville, 2/4th KOYLI on the Seine bridges, and 2/6th Duke of Wellingtons defending the village of Boos east of Rouen. It was these units which bravely attempted to hold up the armour and infantry of 5th and 7th Panzer Divisions as they approached Rouen on the afternoon of the 8th. Despite their lack of suitable weapons they were able to hold up the Germans for three hours, destroying tanks and vehicles and thereby preventing them from occupying Rouen that night. They were then withdrawn across the Seine.

Only that evening orders were received to withdraw IX Corps from the Bresle and General Ihler announced his intention to reach Rouen by the 12th. Given the limited transport of the French units this was not unreasonable, but it ignored the fact that 5th and 7th Panzer Divisions had already reached the outskirts of Rouen and were likely to impede his progress. In fact they occupied Rouen on the morning of the 9th and the fate of IX Corps was sealed by ten German divisions, as there were no more bridges over the Seine beyond Rouen.

Major General Fortune had already begun to move his Division during the night. It was divided into two parts: 'A' and 153 Brigades were carried first to a line covering Dieppe, while 152 and 154 Brigades were moved further south to a line on the Béthune River. By doubling up on all the transport the Division was able to move into position relatively fast, but the French divisions could only manage 20 kilometres a day. During the morning news came that the Germans had already occupied Rouen and it became necessary to change IX Corps' destination from Rouen to Le Havre, from where a naval evacuation could be arranged. In order to protect the move to Le Havre, Fortune decided to send part of the Division encamped around Arques la Bataille to reinforce a defence line covering Le Havre from Fécamp to Lillebonne. This group of units consisting of 'A' and 154 Brigades, plus artillery, engineer and support units, under command of Brigadier Stanley-Clarke, quickly became known as Arkforce. The other origin of the Arkforce name was that 'they had two of everything, and knew that sooner or later they would be going to sea'. Anyway, they moved off promptly during the night of the 9th and proceeded to set up positions south of Fécamp.

51st Highland Division benefited from the fact that German forces facing the Bresle were slow in following up the withdrawal from the river, one of the reasons, without doubt, being that they were held up at two of the crossings by men of D Company of the 4th Border Regiment and A Company of the 1/5th Sherwood Foresters Regiment. These men knew that the task of defending the Bresle River had been given high importance and that they had been ordered to hold their positions. Unfortunately, the order to withdraw did not reach them and despite numerous attempts by the Germans to dislodge them, they stayed at their posts, denying their crossings to the Germans. Only on 13 June, when they were finally persuaded that all fighting north of the Seine had ceased, did they reluctantly surrender. Their fighting performance was a supreme example of doggedness and loyalty to orders.

No sooner had Arkforce left than the German ring began to close. Major General Rommel, with his 7th Panzer Division, was determined to forestall another British evacuation and had cut north from Rouen to the coast. As a result his troops managed to intercept a wireless truck which was on its way to relay communications between Arkforce and 51st Highland Division, just outside Cany on the River Durdent. He then thrust forward to the coast to occupy the small villages of St Sylvain and Le Tot (now the site of a nuclear power station). This area had already been occupied by the 2nd Seaforths, who attempted to stop the panzers, but due to the road congestion the artillery were unable to get forward quickly enough to support them. As a result Rommel's troops were able to gain the western cliffs which overlooked St Valery-en-Caux. From there they could dominate the town and the narrow tidal estuary.

Major General Fortune had intended to move to the Durdent during the night of the 10th/11th on his way to Le Havre, but Lothian Horse reconnaissance showed that the Germans had already begun occupying Veulettes on the coast. He was now convinced that his troops would not be able to reach Le Havre and an evacuation from St Valery-en-Caux should be attempted.

Fortune, whose division was already short of rations and ammunition, benefited from the services of an exceptional naval liaison officer, the redoubtable Commander Elkins, who not only led the preparations for the evacuation, but actually encouraged the British and French soldiers to continue fighting when surrounded. He was eventually captured himself, but escaped from the columns of prisoners and got himself back to England within two weeks.

Admiral Sir William James (Commander-in-Chief Portsmouth) had organized Operation Cycle to lift the base soldiers and fighting men from the Normandy and Brittany ports. Admiral James was short of warships to provide convoy protection and decided to use the few warships he had to patrol the shipping routes, while the large number of cargo and passenger ships he had would use the same routes back to England. James had arrived at Le Havre on the 10th with flotillas of many small and large ships, intending to pick up the French and British soldiers from St Valery-en-Caux, but these plans were upset by sea fog. Given that only the larger ships had wirelesses, it was impossible to organize a move to a port, and then an evacuation, when overlooked by German guns and tanks. Already, on the evening of 10 June, the destroyers *Ambuscade* and *Boadicea* had been damaged by German artillery as they attempted to lift soldiers from the beaches. This problem was compounded as thousands of troops moved into the narrow roads around St Valery-en-Caux, and congestion slowed the troops down and interfered with plans to defend the harbour and town.

St Valery-en-Caux is a small fishing port on the Normandy Coast. It provides one of the few breaks in the high chalk cliffs which march alongside the sea for much of the Normandy coastline. However the roads inside the town are narrow and steep and its approach roads are also very narrow. Within 24 hours some 40,000 allied troops were cramming themselves into the town as they sought refuge from the six German divisions directly ringed around St Valery.

Major General Fortune was convinced that ships would arrive on the night of the 11th or early morning on the 12th to rescue his soldiers. British and French troops were manning a perimeter, but in many places the Germans had broken through making defence very difficult. As a result troops in fighting positions as well as those in the town were bombed, shelled, mortared and fired on through the night. In preparation for the evacuation on the night of the 11th/12th, most of the artillery, anti-tank guns, carriers and tanks had been rendered useless, and when the ships had not appeared the only thing left to do was to organize some infantry attacks in a bid to retake cliffs overlooking the harbour. However, some French troops had already surrendered the previous evening and displayed white flags, making defence difficult. Finally General Ihler ordered a surrender at 0800 hrs on the 12th. Fortune did not feel that he could comply with this order until he was satisfied that there was no possibility of evacuating his soldiers. Finally, at 1100, realizing the vulnerable nature of all the soldiers crowded into St Valery and overlooked by German guns, he ordered the surrender.

During the night of the 11th/12th and the morning of the 12th, some British and French ships came inshore at Veules-les-Roses, an even smaller fishing port east of St Valery. Hundreds of soldiers attempted to flee St Valery and get down to the shore from the cliffs using rifle slings to escape the Germans, and some fell to their deaths. Nevertheless a total of 2,137 British and 1,184 French troops were taken off from the small beach at Veules before the valiant French patrol ship Cérons was grounded and sunk by air attack. The remnants of this ship can still be seen occasionally at low tide – some of its guns were recovered from the wreck and are displayed on the cliff top overlooking the small beach area as a poignant reminder of the desperate attempts to save the French and British troops.

In the meantime Arkforce had got to Le Havre and some 2,222 British troops were evacuated to England during the night of the 13th/14th, while 8,837 were carried around the coast to Cherbourg to continue fighting. However, Lieutenant General Brooke's decision saved them from further combat and eventually some 30,360 men were evacuated from Cherbourg and 21,474 from St Malo.

The surrender of such a famous division was a shock to the Government and without doubt would have been a dramatic piece of news if it had been widely disseminated. As it was, it was not widely publicized, and only emerged as part of a cascade of rumour and bad news which assailed the British people at the time. It has been claimed that the news of the surrender was actually suppressed, although clearly if this was true it was not done very successfully and the truth of what happened to the 51st Highland Division quickly became well known to the families of the Division's many soldiers throughout Scotland. It has also been claimed that the Division was deliberately sacrificed by Churchill to keep the French fighting in the War. He himself lay some of the blame for the loss of the Division on the French High Command because it did not allow the Division to retire towards Rouen when it was possible. Churchill wrote that this movement 'was forbidden by the already disintegrating French Command'. However, Churchill was not being totally logical in blaming the French. He was at the same time decisively involved in sending three more divisions (the last British reserves) to bolster this same 'disintegrating French Command'. Moreover had the 51st Highland Division marched south earlier it might well have been unable to avoid being caught up in the eventual collapse of French forces well away from the coast and there would have been no chance to arrange evacuation. It is equally unfair to blame Major General Fortune for not disengaging from the other slow-moving units of IX Corps and moving swiftly to Le Havre with the whole of his formation. 51st Highland Division certainly had sufficient transport to lift all its units, but that would have meant abandoning the remainder of IX Corps to its fate, having fought closely alongside its units for the previous seven days.

CHAPTER 11

The Missing Commander Finally Appears

Lieutenant General Alan Brooke was ordered to return to Britain from Dunkirk on 30 May. Not unnaturally, he was extremely upset at having to leave II Corps, which he had commanded since arriving in France in October 1939, and which was still assembling for evacuation on the Dunkirk beaches. The BEF had left its defensive positions on the French border and advanced into Belgium as part of the Allied response to the German invasion of Belgium. It had been prepared to defend its front on the River Dyle in Belgium, but was forced to retreat by the collapse of the Belgian Army and the French withdrawals on its flanks. Although II Corps had been able to conduct a reasonably ordered retreat, it had been an ignominious experience. Brooke might perhaps have feared that this was to be his last opportunity to command troops in the field as he handed over command of II Corps to Major General Bernard Montgomery. Up until then, Montgomery had been commanding the 3rd Division very competently, having taken it forward to Brussels, fought the advancing Germans of Bock's Army Group, and then brought it back, virtually intact, to Dunkirk. Montgomery, who was not often given to sentiment, describes Brooke breaking down on the beach as he said goodbye. Montgomery, who was also usually not slow to criticize other generals, had nothing but praise for Brooke's command of II Corps. Certainly this high opinion was shared by others and Brooke was created KCB on his return.

Brooke was particularly commended for his defence of the area around Ypres, which had been opened up to German attack following the surrender of the Belgian Army. To hold this threatened area, Gort had despatched to him the 5th and 50th Divisions. These were the BEF's two reserve divisions which, under the so-called Weygand Plan, should have been used to fight a way through to the south to enable the BEF to link up with the rest of the French Army. However, Montgomery's soldiers had captured a German Staff Order which revealed that the Germans planned to take advantage of the impending Belgian surrender to break through at this point and it was vital to ensure that the BEF was not surrounded. The ensuing successful defence of the area held by the Belgians allowed the British to withdraw their forces to Dunkirk and much of the credit for the success of this operation has been rightly placed to the credit of Brooke and Montgomery.

Nowadays it is sometimes hard to realize that no one, neither friend nor foe, really expected that the whole of the BEF could be evacuated successfully from Dunkirk. Beforehand, when planning for the evacuation began on 19 May, it was anticipated that just a proportion of the British Army, perhaps 40,000 men at best, would be saved. With the Germans pressing hard all around the Dunkirk perimeter, the odds were definitely against a successful evacuation of more than a small percentage of the BEF. Both the Germans and Brooke had expected that the Belgian port of Ostend would be the most suitable to use for an evacuation, but it was effectively lost on 27 May. To the west, the first German troops had reached Gravelines and the Aa Canal by the 24th, although Calais and parts of Boulogne were still in British hands. By the 28th, six panzer divisions and two motorized divisions, plus supporting troops of Army Group A, were pressing against the Canal Line and Army Group B was advancing against the defenders from the east. From 24 May (when von Rundstedt ordered the panzers not to proceed beyond the Canal Line), the attacks by the Luftwaffe on ships and soldiers, and the artillery fire on the beaches and town seemed almost continuous. As it happened, the Allies benefited particularly from the 'Halt Order' and the failure of the Luftwaffe to reduce Dunkirk by air attack, which kept German Army units back from the bomb line. Although six destroyers, eight personnel ships and 200 smaller craft were lost, in the end only some 2,000 men were lost in ships sailing for

England, an amazing figure considering that some 338,000 Allied troops were lifted from the harbour and beaches. Although the RAF was criticized for not providing sufficient air cover, they in fact lost 177 aircraft (destroyed and damaged) over the Dunkirk area, and Churchill was at pains to commend them for their efforts (even though this effort went largely unnoticed by the British troops on the beaches). The Luftwaffe reported some 240 aircraft lost in France and Belgium in the same period.

At the time, Dunkirk was not seen as the end of a chapter, but just an event in the Allied retreat. Many of the 95,000 French soldiers, who were also evacuated from Dunkirk, were taken directly or indirectly to Cherbourg, where they were formed into new divisions ready to be thrown into the continuing struggle. The actual campaign in Belgium and northern France had started just three weeks earlier and although the four northern armies had been surrounded and broken, it was assumed that the remainder of the French Army would continue fighting in the south, and that they would continue to be supported by British forces.

A hasty defence line along the Rivers Somme and Aisne, called the Weygand Line, was improvised as the Germans focussed on reducing the Dunkirk enclave. For the defence of the Weygand Line, the French still had some fifty divisions (including the two British divisions, the 51st Highland and 1st Armoured, and the ten divisions in the Maginot Line).

Gradually Churchill and his War Cabinet began to realize that the French forces might be on the edge of defeat and Churchill wanted to exert every effort to keep them in the war against Germany. For one thing, the British Army had sent almost all its guns, ammunition and heavy equipment to France and, as most of this had been lost in the retreat to Dunkirk, there were very few heavy weapons such as tanks, anti-tank guns and heavy artillery available for Home Defence, and Britain therefore would stand virtually defenceless, if the Germans were free to attack across the Channel. Many, including Churchill, considered it a real possibility that the Germans might decide to invade Britain immediately after Dunkirk was finally taken – after all, they had just successfully invaded seven countries in less than nine months. What was there to stop them launching an immediate sneak attack on say the East Coast of England? Only on later reflection did it become obvious that the strength of the Royal Navy and Royal Air Force, as well as the lack of available German landing craft and support shipping, made this threat rather remote, certainly until at least the RAF had been destroyed by the Luftwaffe. Nevertheless, despite the lack of resources for Home Defence, and even before the evacuation from Dunkirk was complete, the War Office was ordered to plan to create a new BEF to support the French Army.

General Ironside, as the new Commander-in-Chief of the United Kingdom (having been relieved of the job of CIGS), had just managed to ensure that in early June two divisions were fully equipped for Home Defence. However Churchill, in his determination to use every means to support the struggling French Army, was prepared to expend even this slender reserve. On 31 May, he and Clement Atlee attended a meeting of the Supreme War Council in Paris. During this meeting Churchill promised, despite the bad news from the north of France and the evacuation from Dunkirk, the continuing support of British land and air forces. On his return, he sent a memo, on 2 June, to the Chiefs of Staff calling for a reconstitution of the BEF with two/three new divisions to join the two still active in France, and consideration of a plan to create a bridgehead in the Brittany area, particularly if the French Army ceased fighting. The plan for a Breton Redoubt seems to have originated with Prime Minister Reynaud and General de Gaulle, but immediately chimed with Churchill's strong historical sense.

Accordingly, on 2 June, Lieutenant General Alan Brooke was called to the War Office by General Dill, the new CIGS. General Dill told Brooke that he was to command a new II Corps, which was being assembled to reinforce the units still fighting in France. For a commander who had just been forced to abandon his troops on the beaches of Dunkirk this was a wonderful opportunity to strike back at the enemy. However Brooke did not welcome this news. In fact he was totally dismayed by this prospect and later wrote: 'As I look back at the war, this was certainly one of my blackest moments.' For the first time, the reinforcements to be sent against the battle-hardened Germans were due to consist of totally untried troops: a Scottish Territorial division (the 52nd Lowland Division) and the recently arrived Canadian Division, which were in fact the only two fully equipped divisions available in Britain. However, Brooke had made clear his low opinion of Territorial units generally, stating that he believed they could not stand up to attacks by tanks and dive-bombers.

This was an unfair calumny. Very many Territorial units had displayed the utmost pluck and heroism in fighting off heavy German attacks by panzers supported by Stukas – despite the fact that it was often the case that they had not been equipped with adequate anti-tank and anti-aircraft weapons. After all, two thirds of the BEF had been made up of Territorials and reservists, and the sacrifice in obedience to orders of the three Territorial construction divisions has been described earlier. It should not be forgotten that it was two Territorial battalions of the Durham Light Infantry which, together with the remnants of two Royal Tank Regiment battalions, had staged the famous Arras counter-attack which gave the panzers so much trouble on 21 May, and provided a signal example of the vulnerability of the Germans during the early years of the War.

An even more dispassionate assessment was provided by the German VI Corps, which fought the BEF from the Dyle to Dunkirk and produced a report on its fighting abilities (for use by the German Army in its invasion plans):

> The English soldier was in excellent physical condition ... In battle he was tough and dogged. His conviction that England would conquer in the end was unshakable ... The English soldier has always shown himself to be a fighter of high value. Certainly the Territorial divisions are inferior to the Regular troops in training, but where morale is concerned they are their equal.

The second severe disappointment for Brooke was that Dill told him that once sufficient forces had been gathered, General Gort would once again take command of the Second BEF. During the winter of 1939, both Dill and Brooke had served as unhappy corps commanders under Gort, since both considered themselves senior and, in every way, superior to him. In 1938, Gort had been promoted from major general to general as he moved from Commandant of the Staff College to CIGS, as part of the Hore-Belisha purge of older officers. As senior lieutenant generals themselves, both Dill and Brooke had resented Gort's sudden promotion to CIGS and then Commander of the BEF, neither doubting that these were roles for which they were both better qualified. Moreover, after the debacle of retreat culminating in Dunkirk, their opinion of Gort as a field commander had reached a new low. Both felt that he focussed on detail rather than the broad picture. Now Brooke was again expected to take command of another corps under Gort's leadership.

However, Brooke had a third and even more dominant reason for doubting the success of the expedition. With his great knowledge of France he had seen at first hand the shortcomings of the French Army through the winter of 1939: 'I had witnessed the realization of my worst fears concerning its fighting value and morale and now I had no false conceptions as to what its destiny must inevitably be. To be sent back again into that cauldron with a new force to participate in the final stages of French disintegration was indeed a dark prospect.' The dispirited and reluctant General then went to see Anthony Eden, the new Secretary of War, where he made clear his misgivings. 'I wanted him to be quite clear that the expedition ... promised no chances of military success and every probability of disaster.' At least as a result of his strongly expressed misgivings, he did manage to extract the promise of an additional 'Regular' division, which would be ready to join his new Corps by the end of June.

The promised division was to be the 3rd Division, commanded by his old friend Bernard Montgomery, and would be sent in addition to the other two divisions, as soon as it was ready. Brooke actually wanted to take his old 3rd and 4th Divisions, but both could not be got ready in time. Although the 3rd Division had returned almost organizationally intact from France, it had been obliged to leave all its heavy weapons behind. Under Montgomery's leadership it had been considered the best organized of all the BEF's divisions, and was being quickly reorganized and partially re-equipped at its new base in Frome (although it was only able to get one battery of 25-pounder guns). Major General Montgomery was absolutely delighted to be given a clear and important role in returning to France and attacking the Germans. He was so delighted at this news that as soon as he returned to the Division on 6 June, he visited the units and told them personally that there would be no time for leave as they would need to prepare themselves and their equipment for an early return to France. However, the single-minded widower General was astonished at the reception of this news by his men. Many were Regular soldiers who stood there jeering and barracking his news, making it quite clear that after nine months service in France and their narrow escape from the Allied collapse via Dunkirk, they had no greater wish than to go home to prove to their families that they were still alive and well. Montgomery did a rapid rethink and ordered forty-eight hours leave for the whole Division!

On 2 June, the rearguard of British and French troops was still being evacuated from Dunkirk and Lieutenant General Brooke claimed he needed some time to gather together a corps staff. It is instructive to compare the speed of his preparations with those of other officers in a similar position. The retired Lieutenant General Sir Henry Karslake was phoned by the CIGS (Ironside) and told to go to France to take command of the Rear Area troops on 21 May. He accordingly travelled with just two hastily appointed staff officers the following day. An even more interesting comparison is provided some two years later by the appointment to the command of Eighth Army of the ambitious Lieutenant General Montgomery. He flew to Egypt as quickly as he could arrange a flight, travelling with only an ADC, and arriving in Cairo on the morning of 12 August 1942. At a strained meeting with General Auchinleck, the departing Commander-in Chief Middle East Forces (and Commander of Eighth Army), he was ordered not to take over command of Eighth Army until 15 August. Accordingly, early the next morning, 13 August, Montgomery travelled into the desert to meet the Army Staff, and undertake a quick reconnaissance and assessment. Even before eating his lunch he had dismissed the acting Army Commander and forthrightly assumed immediate formal command, thereby deliberately taking command two days earlier than the date that had been specified. But he was aware that the situation in the defensive line at El Alamein was serious and vigorous action was needed if the lives of British soldiers were to be saved. With the Germans likely to attack at any time, the last thing that could be afforded was a power vacuum, although his precipitate action astounded many (particularly Auchinleck!).

One could draw many parallels between the desperate situation in Egypt in August 1942 and that pertaining in France in early June 1940. The 51st Highland Division was part of the French IX Corps and came under command of General Georges. 1st Armoured Division had been worn down to not much more than a regiment by being given impossible tasks by Weygand. The Beauman Division, which was intended for the defence of the British bases, was under the command of Lieutenant General Karslake, yet in the selfless spirit which pertained, Beauman and Karslake used part of Beauman's Division to reinforce 51st Highland Division in order to maintain a defence line against German attacks. Effectively all of these units were still fighting alongside the French Army in France and were sharing its fate. However, the British lacked a senior British field commander to protect their interests as they tried to cope with contradictory French orders and their strength was frittered away in badly organized attacks against strong German positions. Karslake had tried to help them but he, unlike Brooke, was not empowered as the British field commander. Counting these units, other base personnel and RAF support personnel still maintaining aircraft based in France, the lives of almost 150,000 men were at stake. In addition, the 52nd (Lowland) Division and the 1st Canadian Division, as well as Montgomery's 3rd Division, were either landing or making preparations to travel to France as quickly as possible. As these units were the only fully formed and equipped divisions in the UK they were absolutely vital for the continued defence of Britain. Nevertheless, under pressure from Churchill, the War Cabinet had agreed that every effort should be made to support the French in their time of need, and despite the frightful risks, this final reinforcement was being committed to the defence of France.

Lieutenant General Pownall (the former Chief of the General Staff at BEF Headquarters) had been sent by the War Office to see General Weygand, the French Commander, on 6 June to assure him of the speedy arrival of the 52nd and 1st Canadian Divisions and of the 3rd Division, which was due to sail on 22 June. Altogether, with these new troops, there would be six divisions and close to 180,000 British soldiers and airmen based in France, together with huge quantities of military supplies. Given the growing military chaos in France, the fate of this force (equivalent almost to the size of the Eighth Army at El Alamein) was of utmost significance to the survival of the United Kingdom, and it was about to be set adrift in Brittany and Normandy. Writing of these events in later years Winston Churchill mused: 'Looking back on it, I wonder how … we had the nerve to strip ourselves of the remaining effective military formations we possessed.' Given Churchill's often-expressed concern about the eventual fate of the 51st Division, consigned to the care of an already disintegrating French command, some critics might have called this noble gesture foolhardy.

The highly experienced Brooke was clearly a different kind of general to Montgomery. Having been appointed on 2 June, he based himself at Aldershot and lived at home with his wife while he gathered a staff around him. Having expressed very little faith in the military value of the new enterprise, he seemed to be in no hurry to reach France. While he tarried, Lieutenant General Sir Henry Karslake, the temporary GOC of the troops in the Line of Communications area, saw the danger presented by a disintegrating French command structure and continually pressed the CIGS to send the nominated commander to take responsibility for all British troops. Karslake also visited these units frequently. He sympathized with the problems of the 51st Division and 1st Armoured Division as their strength was whittled away in brave but unco-ordinated attacks, but he was powerless to intervene over the British troops who were serving under French command. He could do little more than ensure they received supplies and some reinforcements (from the Beauman Division) while pressing London for the real commander to appear.

Brooke has provided no information about how he proposed to

organize his new command for victory. He kept busy gathering a corps staff and ensuring that he was available to attend the Palace for investiture by the King on 11 June. The only formation of his new command that he visited was the Headquarters of the 1st Canadian Division, which he did for the first time, also on 11 June. During that visit he chaired part of a briefing conference and discussed a draft Operational Instruction for the new Corps. As this meeting was held only the day before 51st Highland Division was actually forced to surrender at St. Valery, it was still assumed that most of 51st Highland Division and 1st Armoured Division would be able to join with the rest of Brooke's new II Corps to defend the Brittany area. The Canadians were told they were due to defend the area around Rennes.

Finally, the new but seemingly reluctant commander left for France on 12 June. When Brooke eventually arrived in Cherbourg on the evening of the 12th, he found that he was not allowed to land until the next morning and expressed his anger over the lack of suitable reception arrangements in his diary: 'And these are the arrangements the War Office has made *after pushing me for a week to get over as quickly as possible*!!' (author's italics). Brooke had just lain down to sleep when Major General Thorpe, the British Commander at Cherbourg, came out to collect him and conduct him to his chateau. This landing occurred in pouring rain and during an air raid on Cherbourg, which provided a less than propitious welcome for Brooke's return to France.

Given that the Second BEF was withdrawn so precipitately from Normandy and Brittany a controversy arose over the seriousness and true extent of the plan for a 'Breton Redoubt'. Apparently the outline plan for the Breton Redoubt was to hold a north–south line across the base of the peninsula from St Nazaire through Rennes to Pontorson. It was assumed that an army based there could be used to threaten any advance by the Germans towards the Loire. Although the new BEF anticipated having five or six divisions available for this task, it would certainly have been difficult to hold such a large area with this force and threaten such an aggressive enemy as the Germans. However, in early June, the French could still have provided additional divisions from the Tenth Army, which was falling back towards Normandy and Brittany, and from other forces in the area. Furthermore, all the major French ports had fortifications and were still manned by strong garrisons. Brittany was not good tank country and the terrain offered defensive capabilities, as did the large towns and bases at Lorient and Brest. In principle, the flanks could have been protected by the Royal Navy and the French Navy, and with good ports available around its coast, particularly at Brest, an Anglo-French Army could have been resupplied from the sea.

As mentioned earlier, the 'Breton Redoubt; was undoubtedly an idea which appealed to Churchill. It chimed with his strong historical perspective and knowledge of how Wellington had baited the French from behind the security of the 'Torres Vedras' lines in Portugal during the Napoleonic Wars. At that time the small Anglo-Portuguese Army had been supplied by the Royal Navy, while the French Army was drained by shortages of supplies coming via long and difficult lines of communication through a seething, occupied Spain. However, in endorsing this idea, Churchill failed to see that fundamental conditions for a successful defence of Brittany were not in place.

In 1940, Allied politicians still needed to gain an understanding of the critical impact of modern air forces on the battlefield, both on land and at sea. Brittany was not as remote as it had been in the eighteenth century and the Germans would have been able to base huge numbers of aircraft on relatively local airfields, from which it would have been easy to attack the defenders and their naval support. Within months, the British were able to demonstrate the ability of even relatively primitive carrier-borne aircraft to cripple the Italian Navy in its most secure base at Taranto. Undoubtedly, the Royal Navy, in trying to support the troops in a Brittany Redoubt, would have been exposed to severe losses, as it was to experience vividly in the disastrous Greek campaign and the evacuation to and from Crete.

Churchill had discussed the Brittany bridgehead in the Paris meeting with Prime Minister Reynaud on 31 May and mentioned it in his memo to the Chiefs of Staff on 2 June. Indeed it was a frequent topic of conversation in London during the early days of June.

Apparently General de Gaulle, who, as the new Deputy Secretary of War, came to London on 8 June to plead for more troops and more fighter aircraft, admitted that he had been in favour of the idea originally. On the War Cabinet Meeting of 11 June, the CIGS was informed 'that a study was being made for organizing a bridgehead to secure Brittany in the event of co-ordinated defence of France becoming impossible, due to the present line breaking'.

Reynaud had already ordered Weygand to begin the creation of the Redoubt on 31 May, as a result of which Weygand had put General René Altmayer (younger brother of General Robert Altmayer commanding Tenth Army) in charge of the project. Work had commenced on some defensive features and some of the four divisions of French troops who had been evacuated from Dunkirk to Cherbourg were being earmarked for its defence. However, Weygand (who seemed to dislike any plan that was not his own), was not in favour of the idea and had to be reminded by Reynaud of the necessity to do something on 6 June. Equally Dill, the new CIGS, seems to have been resolutely against the plan. Major General Spears says that he and Dill argued about the lack of effort by the British to support the plan, after a dinner held on 10 June at Churchill's home. During that heated discussion, Dill had produced one really strong argument against the Redoubt, namely the tremendous strain it would impose on the RAF, whose bases in England were too distant for fighters to cover the peninsula.

Four years later, in August 1944, the Germans had used the intervening time to build strong defences around the major Brittany ports. When the Americans broke through at Avranches on 1 August, they quickly bottled up four German divisions in Brittany. These German forces had virtually no air or naval support. Nevertheless, it took the Americans 10,000 casualties and seven weeks to reduce Brest, and the German garrisons at Lorient and St Nazaire, although surrounded and cut off from resupply, did not surrender until May 1945. (Meanwhile, the 51st Highland Division took a strongly defended Le Havre in three days, with very limited casualties.)

Clearly in June 1940, the line from St Nazaire to Pontorson (near le Mont-St. Michel and Avranches) had few fortifications and was nothing like the original 'Torres Vedras' on which thousands of workers had laboured for a year from 1809 to 1810. Moreover, Wellington did not have to contend with an enemy possessing overwhelming air power operating from nearby airfields. It is therefore quite clear that the defence of an unprepared Brittany in 1940 would have been very difficult and could have led to a catastrophic disaster for Britain. The Germans, after dealing with the rest of the French Army, would have been able to establish good support facilities and could have brought up massive reinforcements to deal with the defenders of the Breton Redoubt at their leisure.

They might even have chosen to exploit the Allied desire to maintain the Breton bridgehead as a means to wear down Britain's Naval and Air Forces as they ran the gauntlet of German submarines and mines, as well as fighter and bomber aircraft. Instead of fighting the Battle of Britain advantageously in the skies over England, the Royal Air Force, operating without radar at the full extent of its range over Brittany, could have suffered a severe drubbing by the Luftwaffe. Even worse, the Germans could have used just a portion of their troops to bottle up the Allied forces in Brittany, while their main force could have been used to invade a severely weakened Britain. Thus Britain, not Germany, could have faced the unpleasant prospect of fighting a war on two fronts. No longer protected by a powerful Navy and Air Force, poorly trained and under-equipped British land forces might have found themselves trying to cope with growing numbers of well-equipped invaders, while what was left of their best-equipped troops were bottled up in Brittany.

The reality was that in June 1940, the overwhelming size of German ground forces and the superiority in available German air power would have bled the Allied forces severely and an eventual forced evacuation from, say Brest, would have been inevitable. Moreover, the fortuitous conditions, such as the Rundstedt/Hitler 'Halt Order', benign weather and a short sea crossing, which favoured the British at Dunkirk, could hardly have been repeated. More likely it would have been a choice between hapless surrender, as at St Valery, or multiple tragedies, replaying the sinking of the RMT *Lancastria*, on the long sea crossing from Brittany to Britain.

Did the brilliant Brooke anticipate all these dire consequences of attempting to hold the Breton Redoubt, or did he, perhaps as Churchill alleged, have cold feet? At Aldershot, Brooke had gathered a Corps staff and set them to planning the defence of the Brittany area. Although the plan had drawbacks, the Breton Redoubt was the only plan on the table. Before leaving England, Brooke had obviously planned to position II Corps around the Rennes area and eventually to bring the British elements, currently with Tenth Army, under II Corps control and use them to defend the Breton Peninsula. In June 1940, France still had strong naval and air forces. Initially the Government (particularly Churchill) intended that in the event of the collapse of French resistance in metropolitan France, a toehold would be retained and would support a France continuing to fight against the Germans from its colonies.

General Dill, the CIGS, had also been formally notified on 11 June about the plan to secure Brittany in the event that the French line broke and sent a message about this plan to Brooke so that Lieutenant General Marshall-Cornwall (liaison officer with 10th Army) could be associated with this 'study'. The draft Operation Order, which Brooke discussed with the Canadians on 11 June, clearly anticipated defending a Brittany bridgehead with British and Canadian troops. Dill was also party to the talks at the Inter-Government Conference at Briare on 11 and 12 June, where the plan for a Breton Redoubt was once again discussed. In any event, according to Major General Spears, he and Dill argued about the plan in London on 10 June. Thus the ramifications of the Breton Redoubt plan could not have been a surprise to Brooke as he left for France on 12 June.

Accordingly, on 14 June, at the end of his meeting with Generals Weygand and Georges, Brooke signed a Memorandum confirming the employment of British troops in defence of Brittany. It beggars belief that the perspicacious Brooke would have put his signature to a plan for the employment of his Corps in the defence of the Breton Redoubt, unless he believed this was the general intention of his own Government. Brooke, who had been born in France, spoke fluent French, and his discussion with Weygand and Georges covering the military situation should not have suffered from any linguistic misunderstandings. Apart from establishing the Brittany Redoubt, it must have been clear to him that neither of the French generals had any plan to achieve anything except continual withdrawal. It is strange that a man who did not hesitate to argue with the formidable Churchill would have agreed so meekly to an ally's plan which he thought had no chance of success.

Later Brooke claimed that Weygand had informed him that organized resistance by the French Army had come to an end (although this was later denied by Weygand). That organized French resistance was collapsing seems undoubted, but Brooke seems to have ignored the positive news of the withdrawal of the remnants of the Tenth Army into Brittany, which would undoubtedly have provided further French divisions to assist in defence of the Brittany Redoubt.

Brooke, albeit reluctantly, went to France to lead a new BEF committed to fighting alongside the French Army. The Second BEF was due to comprise a Corps Headquarters and four fully formed infantry divisions (51st Highland, 52nd Lowland, 1st Canadian, and later Montgomery's 3rd Division) as well as the remnants of 1st Armoured Division and Beauman's Division. Immediately after the meeting with the French generals Brooke seems to have had a new perception of the military situation. Was it the shock of the news of the loss of the 51st or the sight of the Supreme French Commander worrying about the effect of the disaster on his career, and the knowledge that neither Weygand nor Georges controlled events any longer? Brooke certainly seems to have been galvanized from his previous sloth and determined to change his orders before a huge military disaster overwhelmed his forces. Despite having signed the Memorandum, he immediately drafted a message for the CIGS, saying that the three generals were all agreed as to the impossibility of holding Brittany with the troops available and recommending that the two military missions be closed, as Weygand and Georges would no longer be in command of their armies. He then sent Major General Howard-Vyse back to London with his memo and a copy of the agreement, which he had signed with Weygand and Georges.

Clearly he thought the changed situation important enough to use a general as his courier.

It is difficult to understand the complete contrast between what Brooke had agreed with the two French generals and the message he sent back to London just a few hours later. It appears Brooke anticipated the total collapse of French defence within days, and thus the total impossibility of holding a bridgehead in France with what was left of the Second BEF. That afternoon as soon as Brooke got back to the British L of C Headquarters at Le Mans, he telephoned General Dill and asked for clarification of the decision regarding the Breton Redoubt. Dill, as mentioned earlier, was strongly against the plan and then spoke to Churchill, reportedly later telling Brooke that Churchill knew nothing of such a plan. This was clearly not true for Churchill had been enamoured with the plan since it had been first broached. Churchill understood the necessity of supporting the French (particularly Reynaud) against those elements of his Cabinet who wanted an armistice. The previous day, after a late-night phone call from Reynaud, Churchill, at great personal risk, had flown once again to France and met with Reynaud at Tours. The object of this last inter-governmental meeting was to dissuade the French from seeking an armistice and to ensure that the French Fleet did not fall into the clutches of the Germans.

Brooke's apologists make much of the fact that there was no formal plan for the defence of Brittany, only an intent to create a study of the idea. As such, their arguments amount to splitting hairs over verbs. The French however, had begun defensive works in some areas. Clearly Churchill felt constrained when he wrote his memoirs not to reveal how firm the plan was, but he could not hide his disappointment that it was not carried out. Perhaps Franco-British relations might have been better in later years if more of an attempt had been made to defend Brittany, but it would undoubtedly have been at a high price.

What actually changed Brooke's mind? Having lived through the nightmare of a well-organized British Army being forced to retreat in disorder by events outside its control, Brooke clearly did not want to repeat this experience with his new II Corps. Only when he arrived in France did he discover that his key division (the well-equipped 51st Highland Division) had already been lost. Notably, Brooke seems to have suffered very little concern over the fact that if he had come out earlier and taken the 51st under direct command, he might have saved it!

Lieutenant General Brooke was an extremely experienced artillery officer and must have been painfully aware of the significance of the loss of not just one third of the infantry force he needed to defend Brittany, but a major part of the artillery assets he was expecting to command. 51st Highland Division had suffered casualties and losses during its retreat, but its original artillery complement had been far larger than those of any of the divisions which Brooke expected to land shortly from the UK. Its artillery had included 1st RHA, 17th, 23rd and 75th Field Regiments, 51st Anti-Tank Regiment and particularly 51st Medium Regiment Royal Artillery. In addition it had two machine-gun regiments. Some of these units got away with Arkforce, but Brooke would have recognized only too clearly the immense difficulty of conducting a defensive campaign without strong artillery, and he now faced the prospect of defending Brittany with very limited British artillery support.

When describing later his long difficult conversation with Churchill he claimed that he knew that many British soldiers would be lost if he followed Churchill's desire to continue supporting the French, and he had to use all his self-control to avoid losing his temper with Churchill. A more obedient general might have buckled under to Churchill (as many others did) and followed the plan regardless of the consequences – after all, that is what generals are supposed to do!

It is obvious that as an experienced artillery staff officer, Brooke knew that he would have no chance of success without adequate artillery. He mentions that he kept looking at his artillery commander, Kennedy, while arguing with Churchill. True enough, the Canadians had just been equipped with seventy-two new 25-pounder guns (enough for three regiments of artillery), but how much time had they had for training with those guns and exercising their resupply, and how effective would they have been when hammered day and night by Stuka dive-bombing attacks?

However, when he arrived at the British Rear Area Headquarters at Le Mans, at 1400 hrs on 13 June, Brooke received the bombshell of the news of the loss of the 51st Division.

Later there seems to have been a desire, or even a conspiracy, to deny the very existence of a Brittany plan. The official historian, Major Ellis, supports the claim there was in existence no real plan to defend Brittany. However Butler, in his account, *Grand Strategy*, rightly observes that Brooke, in his official despatch, quoting that neither Dill nor Churchill was aware of a Brittany plan, was not strictly correct. Brooke also claimed in his diary that Dill said that he knew nothing of such a plan. This claim was made despite the fact that Dill had just returned from the Briare Conference where Churchill discussed the plan with Reynaud. Moreover Dill had repeated arguments about the merits of the plan with Spears on 10 June! Perhaps it was politic later for all concerned to present a united front and deny that serious consideration had ever been given to this abandoned plan. However, as Spears pointedly asked in his account of the Fall of France, if there was no serious prospect of defending Brittany, then 'why were we landing our precious divisions there as fast as we could?' Churchill confirms in his account of the Second World War that he had agreed with Prime Minister Reynaud at Briares on 11 June 'to draw a kind of "Torres Vedras line" across the foot of the Brittany peninsula'. Churchill felt that the bridgehead might have only been able to hold out for no more than a few weeks against concentrated German attack, but those few weeks would have maintained contact between Britain and France, and enabled large French withdrawals to the South of France and then North Africa. Churchill could clearly see that the only other alternative for the French was surrender and he wrote defensively: 'Let none, therefore, mock at the conception of a bridgehead in Brittany.'

On his return to London, Brooke had much to explain. His Government had sent him with specific instructions to assist the French. He had then signed a commitment with its leading Allied generals, Weygand and Georges, to defend Brittany. This in itself was quite extraordinary. Did the French generals doubt the commitment of the British General without an additional written agreement? Their concerns were clearly not misplaced, as Brooke began to take steps to change his orders almost as soon as he left the meeting.

As the War Cabinet met on 14 June, they had much bad news to digest. Ambassador Kennedy had conveyed the lack of real support from Roosevelt, thereby destroying the last hope of the French. All the news from France was dismal; the Germans had marched into Paris that morning. The War Cabinet knew that only by committing fresh troops and aircraft could they bolster what remained of French resistance. The decision was therefore taken to continue despatching fresh troops, although it was agreed to withdraw Lines of Communication personnel from the French bases and depots (although the Cabinet did not explain how the Army was to fight without having supplies from the depots delivered to it).

At that point General Dill joined the War Cabinet, bringing with him Brooke's telegram. Dill then received a telephone call directly from Brooke in which the latter explained what he had done with the 52nd (Lowland) Division. Dill pointed out that this was not what the Prime Minister wanted him to do, to which Brooke responded, 'What the hell does he want?' Dill replied, 'He wants to speak to you,' and therewith handed the phone over to Churchill. There followed a long and undoubtedly acrimonious conversation between the General and the Prime Minister, as Churchill vainly urged Brooke to help the French feel that the British were supporting them. As Brooke had seen clearly it was impossible to make a corpse feel, and as the French Army was to all intents and purposes dead, he could see no military purpose in sacrificing the 52nd Division and the other divisions of the Second BEF. Brooke seems to have laid the blame for the loss of the 51st Highland Division squarely on Churchill. Apparently at one stage in the conversation Brooke argued, 'You've lost one Scottish Division. Do you wish to lose another?' Clearly Churchill did take some blame for the loss of the 51st, but he could equally have claimed that the Division was lost because Brooke was so tardy in moving to France and taking control of all British troops.

At the end of this exhausting argument, which according to

Brooke took about thirty minutes, Churchill finally agreed with him (it was, according to Brooke, the only time during the War when he actually used the words 'All right, I agree with you'). No wonder Churchill fought hard for his plan. He saw the defence of the Breton Redoubt as the only viable way to provide concrete support to the French at that time and everything hinged on the Second BEF continuing to make a contribution to the defence of France. Yet the man Churchill had sent to achieve this was not prepared to support one of his pet projects, which must have been an unpleasant surprise for him. Undoubtedly he used the full force of his considerable personality to try to convince Brooke to fight on, but Brooke had been a senior general for many years and was not used to having his courage or tactical assessments questioned. As Brooke later recorded, he had difficulty keeping his temper and resisting Churchill's forceful arguments: 'The strength of his power of persuasion had to be experienced to realize the strength that was required to counter it.'

Churchill had been thwarted in the only plan there was to strike back against the Germans and keep the disintegrating French in the War. However, he remembered the conversation somewhat differently and, magnanimously as ever in his written works, recorded: 'I could hear quite well and after ten minutes I was convinced that he was right and we must go.' Brooke however wrote that he was exhausted by an argument that had clearly taken considerably longer than ten minutes.

The Cabinet had the example of the loss of the 51st Division just two days before as a clear warning of the danger of leaving British troops exposed in France. It was then speedily agreed that the Canadians, who had just disembarked, should be re-embarked, but the two remaining brigades of the 52nd Division, which were on their way to join the Tenth Army, should 'be put into the battle if the French were continuing to fight'.

It is clear that Brooke was dilatory in getting himself and an organized British command structure to France. As a result thousands of British soldiers were left to fight under conflicting French orders and were consequently either killed or captured (although it should not be forgotten that at the same time many tens of thousands of French soldiers were sacrificed in equally futile attempts to stop the German advance, while their leaders debated how best to surrender). In the event Brooke saw more clearly than Churchill and the War Cabinet that nothing could be achieved in the conditions of June 1940. To send more troops to support a disintegrating France was to reinforce defeat, at a calamitous cost for Britain. In the event Brooke did demonstrate his ability to organize a 'just in time' evacuation for the remaining British personnel, which resulted in many tens of thousands of men being brought back to the UK where they could continue the struggle against Germany.

In so doing Brooke did a great service to the defence of Britain, although he certainly could have done much more to backload the precious stocks of guns and tanks needed for such a massive undertaking.

CHAPTER 12

Operation Cycle

The Evacuation from the Normandy Ports

Brooke had his fateful discussion with Churchill on the evening of 14 June. Even before that conversation he had given orders for the disembarkation of parts of the 52nd Lowland Division to stop and for the Canadians to re-embark. By later that evening he had received a confirmatory order from Eden that he was no longer under French Command and should prepare for withdrawal to the UK. A desperate struggle then began to get as many units and men out of France as quickly as possible. Brooke handed over command of all the British troops with French Tenth Army to Lieutenant General Marshall-Cornwall (these troops were now called 'Normanforce'), who was ordered to co-operate with the French in any actual fighting, but also to make his way to Cherbourg for evacuation. The fighting primarily involved 157 Brigade of the 52nd Lowland Division, which had been placed under direct command of the French Tenth Army, and accordingly met the Germans in rearguard actions at Conches and Mortagne. Finally, on 17 June, 157 Brigade received orders to disengage, got into its transport and headed for Cherbourg. A small number of tanks, scout cars and forty-nine lorries from 1st Armoured Division also drove the 200 miles to Cherbourg (although they lost the tanks which they had loaded on a train without escorts). They were all embarked by the evening of the 17th.

Brooke had landed in France early on 13 June and five days later, on the evening of the 17th, he boarded the armed trawler *Cambridgeshire* in St Nazaire, for the return to England. The *Cambridgeshire* acted as escort for a slow convoy and he did not reach Southampton until the evening of the 19th. For a general, of

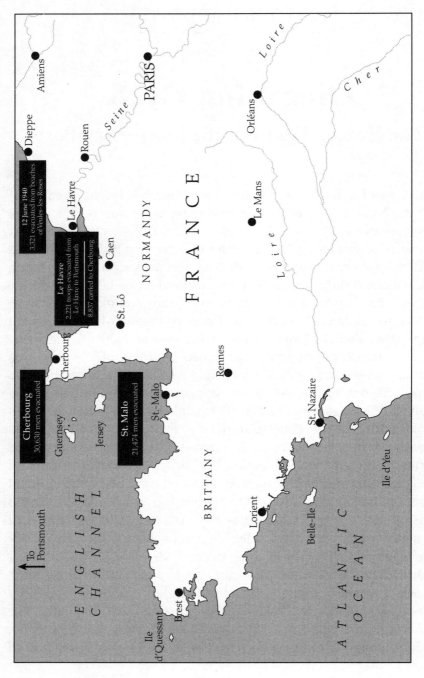

To Portsmouth

ENGLISH CHANNEL

Cherbourg
30,630 men evacuated

Guernsey

Jersey

St. Malo
21,474 men evacuated

St. Malo

Ile d'Quessant

Brest

BRITTANY

Lorient

Belle-Ile

ATLANTIC OCEAN

Ile d'Yeu

Rennes

St. Nazaire

12 June 1940
3,321 evacuated from beaches
of Veules-les-Roses

Le Havre
2,221 troops evacuated from
Le Havre to Portsmouth
8,837 carried to Cherbourg

Dieppe

Rouen

Le Havre

Caen

St. Lô

NORMANDY

Seine

PARIS

Amiens

Loire

Orléans

Le Mans

Loire

Cher

F R A N C E

Map 5. Operation Cycle – Evacuation of Second BEF from Normandy.

whom so much was expected, to return so quickly and ignominiously to Britain, it was a great disappointment. On his arrival at the War Office on the morning of the 20th he was castigated for not having brought back more guns and vehicles. Had the CIGS, General Dill, not been a very close friend and supporter, it is quite certain that the career of this distinguished officer, who had dared to stand up to the Prime Minister, might have been ended at this point. He was fortunate that the final closure of the Second BEF chapter was on the whole so successful. Not only were the precious Canadian and Lowland Divisions saved, but so were parts of the 51st Highland, Beauman and 1st Armoured Divisions, as well as tens of thousands of other Army and Air Force personnel. The British were also able to rescue sizeable numbers of French, Polish and Czechoslovakian troops who went on to form the nucleus of some extremely valuable fighting formations. In addition, the terrible catastrophe which overtook the *Lancastria*, as we shall see, although initially concealed from the general public, provided a clear example of what might have happened if the British had dallied any longer.

Most of the German Army was involved in fighting the remnants of the French Army, which although facing almost certain defeat, were if anything fighting even harder as they retreated through central France. To most Germans, the action in Brittany and Normandy were therefore mere sideshows, although this was not the case for the ambitious Rommel and his 7th Panzer Division. He boasted that he had captured 40,000 soldiers and eleven generals at St Valery-en-Caux, and although he described the occupation of Normandy as almost a peaceful 'lightning tour of France', his determination to follow up swiftly his victory at St Valery caught the French defenders unprepared, and forced the British to evacuate even faster than they had planned. While he completed the occupation of the Normandy peninsula, 5th Panzer Division began occupying Brittany.

The ships of Admiral James's Operation Cycle had been unable to rescue 51st Highland Division from St Valery. However, they were successful in picking up several thousand men from Veules-les-Roses and Arkforce was evacuated from Le Havre. Eventually, a total of 30,630 men of Normanforce (mostly 52nd Lowland Division) and others were evacuated from Cherbourg, as well as 21,474 (mainly from 1st Canadian Division) who were evacuated from St Malo. Royal Navy demolition parties also tried to make sure that vital installations were not left intact for the Germans to use and the ports were left wreathed in smoke as the Royal Navy steamed away.

According to Rommel, the defence of Cherbourg caused him some concern, due to the potential strength of the defenders. However, it is quite clear that no real defence was offered by the well-built harbour fortifications, which, after a token defence against virtually the reconnaissance elements of 7th Panzer Division, promptly surrendered. Marshall-Cornwall stated that he ordered 5th Battalion, KOSB and five battalions of the Cherbourg garrison to establish a blocking position at St Sauveur (about 20 miles due south of Cherbourg) to enable stores and vehicles to be loaded on the ships until 21 June. However, on the morning of 18 June, sixty lorries carrying motorized German infantry (from 7th Panzer Division) began approaching the outer defence line. They were blocked by the Scots at St Sauveur, but were able to outflank them by taking the western coastal road, where the French troops offered little resistance. Marshall-Cornwall ordered the Scots to pull back to Cherbourg, embark and sail by 1600 hrs. His report concludes that when they left, the Germans were still 3 miles from Cherbourg. Nevertheless, the French Navy did undertake substantial demolitions of warships and submarines, which were under construction at the Cherbourg naval yards.

Rommel, determined to make his reputation, made sure that his successes were recorded by the newsreel cameramen from the Propaganda Ministry who accompanied him and by his personal Leica (a gift from Goebbels), which was often hung around his neck. Nevertheless, although his Division occupied Normandy fairly rapidly and took some 8,000 British troops prisoner, the Royal Navy (including some French ships) ensured that more than 50,000 men were rescued to fight another day.

Rommel had pushed his Division hard, from the front, to make rapid advances, and 7th Panzer Division was involved in many bloody engagements, including the Dinant crossing, the British counter-attack at Arras, the capture of Lille (against five French divisions, namely half of the French First Army), and then the crossing of the Somme and advance into Normandy. Nevertheless, its casualty list was comparatively modest. For the six-week campaign it recorded 682 killed, 1,646 wounded and 296 missing. Although 7th Panzer Division was a 'light division' with just one tank regiment (the 25th Tank Regiment, which had an establishment of three battalions each with about seventy-five tanks, mostly Czech), due to the efficiency of its three mobile workshops, which quickly recovered and repaired damaged tanks, just forty-two tanks were eventually reported totally destroyed. Therefore less than 20 per cent of 7th Panzer Division's tanks were lost in the short but arduous campaign in which it played such a central role. This, in spite of the fact that, as mentioned earlier, Rommel had initially lost so many tanks in his rapid advance from Dinant that he was forced to amalgamate his three battalions, and was given command of the two tank regiments from 5th Panzer Division for his successful attack on Lille on 26 May. The strength and durability of German tanks and their crews (supported by the ability of their intrepid recovery engineers) was to stand Rommel in good stead during the coming two years of desert warfare, which was to crown his growing reputation as a soldier

CHAPTER 13

Operation Aerial

Evacuation from the Atlantic Ports and the Loss of HMT *Lancastria* at St Nazaire

Despite the multiple difficulties which are involved in the evacuation of a whole army by sea, the British evacuations were, on the whole, blessed with good luck. The combination of good luck, intrepid seamanship and good weather enabled the Royal Navy to organize its own and Allied ships to evacuate almost all those who wanted to leave France. It could have been a very different story. Timing was everything, as proved by the rapid encirclement of the 51st Highland Division on 11 June, which prevented its evacuation by sea, while Arkforce, which set off for Le Havre just the night before, was saved. Also, the substantial bomb damage to ships, including the disaster which befell the *Lancastria* at St Nazaire, showed how narrow was the margin between success and disaster, and how easily much more of the Second BEF and its support troops could have been lost.

The debacle of the destruction of the Allied armies in northern France had taken centre stage during May, but by 14 June ships began unloading Allied troops in Brest, who were arriving back after the failure to hold Norway. With its long coastline, difficult land communications and easy sea access Norway would have been a far better location from which to pursue a 'redoubt defence', but the Allies had already failed there. Nevertheless, the French Government broadcast its intention to continue fighting from a redoubt in Brittany, and French troops began manning two rings of poorly prepared defence lines around Brest under the command of General Charbonneau, while Weygand and Georges began planning with Brooke the utilization of the new British divisions in Brittany.

Map 6. Operation Aerial – Evacuation of Second BEF and other troops from Brittany and the Atlantic Coast.

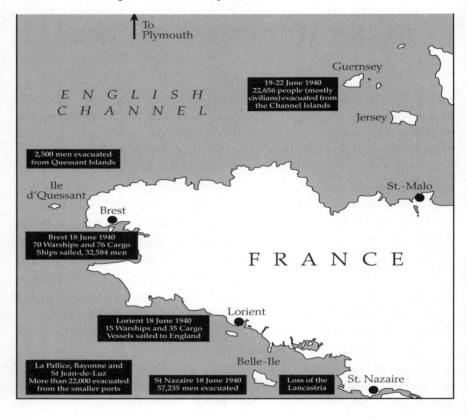

To Plymouth

ENGLISH CHANNEL

Guernsey

19-22 June 1940
22,656 people (mostly civilians) evacuated from the Channel Islands

Jersey

2,500 men evacuated from Quessant Islands

Ile d'Quessant

St.-Malo

Brest

Brest 18 June 1940
70 Warships and 76 Cargo Ships sailed, 32,584 men

FRANCE

Lorient

Lorient 18 June 1940
15 Warships and 35 Cargo Vessels sailed to England

Belle-Ile

La Pallice, Bayonne and St Jean-de-Luz
More than 22,000 evacuated from the smaller ports

St Nazaire 18 June 1940
57,235 men evacuated

Loss of the Lancastria

St. Nazaire

At the same time the opportunity to do something was passing quickly. Paris had been declared an 'open city', and was occupied without a shot on 14 June. Having broken through the crust of the Weygand Line, the seemingly invincible Wehrmacht raced pell-mell through France, heading for the Atlantic coast and the Swiss border. On 17 June the 84-year-old Maréchal Pétain, who had the previous day taken over as the new President of France after the resignation of Reynaud, had opened negotiations for armistice terms with the German High Command, and made a radio appeal to French troops to lay down their arms. France's First World War 'Hero of Verdun', who was always of a pessimistic nature, was about to lead his nation into co-existence with the Germans, and to lose all the territories regained at the end of the First World War.

In England, on 14 June 1940, the decision was made to launch the evacuation of any remaining Allied troops from the western French ports. For the evacuation of the Second BEF from Brittany and the ports of western France, the Royal Navy, under Admiral Sir Martin Dunbar-Nasmith (Commander-in-Chief of Britain's Western Approaches at Plymouth) had ordered the beginning of a new evacuation operation, codenamed 'Operation Aerial'. Among the many ships that were gathered to evacuate the troops and civilians from Brittany was the former Cunard White Star Liner, the 16,243-ton HMT *Lancastria*. Built in 1922 on the Clyde by William Beardmore and Co, the *Lancastria* had originally been named the *Tyrrhenia*, but apparently this was not a lucky choice as the ship quickly acquired the nickname of the 'Soup Tureen'. In 1924, she was given a refit and a new name. As RMS *Lancastria* she was a popular cruise ship, being used for Atlantic crossings and then the cruising market until War came, when she was taken up from trade and converted to a troop and cargo ship.

In April 1940, she carried Canadian troops to Britain from Iceland and then, on her return in May, the *Lancastria* was used to bring troops back from Harstad in Norway. During this long and extremely dangerous journey she was attacked by high-flying aircraft, but fortunately their bombs missed the ship. On 12 June 1940, the *Lancastria* was moved to a Liverpool shipyard for refitting. Barely had she entered port and her crew sent on leave, when she received the order to join Operation Aerial. The dispersed crew were quickly gathered and the *Lancastria* set course for Plymouth on 14 June 1940 and then sailed on for Brittany's Quiberon Bay. Arriving in the small hours of the morning on 16 June, Captain Sharp found his ship to be superfluous to the rescue operations in Lorient and, accompanied by the 20,341-ton liner *Franconia*, was ordered to move onwards to St Nazaire that evening. As they approached the coast, an evening bombing attack damaged the *Franconia*, so the *Lancastria* entered the mouth of the Loire estuary alone. The *Lancastria* was too large to enter the actual port, thus at 0400 hrs on the morning of the 17th, Captain Sharp brought his ship to anchor in 12 fathoms of water at Charpentier Roads near the harbour's entrance, some 5 miles off St Nazaire.

On shore at St Nazaire, thousands of men were queuing up waiting for boats to take them out to the big troopships lying anchored offshore. Three RNVR officers came on board the *Lancastria* to determine how many could be loaded and Captain Sharp was asked how many passengers he could take. His normal complement, including a crew of some 330, was 2,180. However, he had brought some 2,653 soldiers back from Norway, so he indicated that he could take 3,000 'at a pinch'. The senior RNVR officer apparently responded by stating that he would have to take as many as he possibly could, 'without regard to the limits of International Law'. The ship had some sixteen lifeboats (which Captain Sharp later ordered swung out when the bombing began) but in the event it seems that there were only enough lifejackets for some 2,500 passengers, although at least twice as many men were loaded on the ship. In his official report, Captain Sharp stated 'not everyone who had a lifebelt was saved ... I should estimate that 2,000 were saved by lifebelts and another 500 in boats and rafts, so that 2,500 people were saved out of a total of about 5,500. I lost 70 of my crew of 330.'

Later it was estimated that the number who came on board was far in excess of the 'official figure' of 5,000 and some survivors claimed there were 7,000 or even 9,000 passengers crowded into the holds and cabins of the ship. In view of the subsequent tragedy, the British

Government would have found it inconvenient to admit that perhaps it had responsibility for overloading the ship, as the result of which so many men were lost. Perhaps, therefore, it was convenient later to appear uncertain how many passengers were actually loaded. Some survivors claimed that after they had loaded over 4,000 men, the loading officers stopped counting, although this is difficult to believe. Loading the ship was a military operation organized by responsible officers – there was only one way to get onto the ship and the Royal Navy knew how to count. For example, Major Morgan reported that he ferried some 242 men of his 663 Artisan Works Company, Royal Engineers out to the *Lancastria*. The ship was already crowded with men and a loading officer shouted down to Morgan that the vessel had over 7,200 men aboard and could take no more. Morgan immediately shouted back up that another 242 weren't going to make any difference and they climbed aboard. He reported that out of his 242 men, more than 90 were lost in the tragedy that day.

Bodies were packed into the ship wherever there was room. For example, when Major Scott-Bowden of the 53rd Company, Auxiliary Pioneer Corps, boarded with his men from the destroyer HMS *Havelock*, it was apparent to him that the *Lancastria* was becoming overcrowded with men. Once on board he was instructed by the ship's Purser to proceed to a second-class cabin which had four bunk beds, but soon discovered that seven other officers were meant to be in the same accommodation. He quickly returned to the Purser who replied: 'Sorry Sir, but that's the best I can do. You're lucky to get a bunk at all. Three men will have to sleep on the floor and two of those are Colonels!' Among those who came on board early that morning were Royal Air Force ground crew from squadrons (particularly 73 and 98 Squadrons) of the Advanced Air Striking Force. Perhaps as many as 2,000 RAF men were crowded into the spacious No. 1 and No. 2 holds. Also on board were some civilians who had been working for Fairey Aviation in Belgium, plus a number of French civilians, including women and children.

During the morning and afternoon, as the ship rolled gently at its anchor, boats came out to the ship and continued to embark passengers, while a number of bombing attacks were made by the Luftwaffe. Ships are notoriously difficult targets to hit from the air, particularly if they are moving. However, although the *Lancastria* was at anchor, its luck held until at about 1550 hrs, when several Ju 88 twin-engined bombers from KG30 (KampfGeschwader 30, a Luftwaffe unit which had specialized in shipping targets) arrived to begin their attacks. *Lancastria* had steam up and was ready to sail as soon as it received orders, but it was still lying stationary in the afternoon sun. Despite attempts being made to hold them off with Bren-gun fire, one bomber was finally successful and struck the *Lancastria*. Its four bombs were seen to straddle the ship.

Many eyewitnesses have claimed that during this attack on the *Lancastria* they saw one of the bombs going directly down the funnel. However, according to Frank Brogden, an engineering officer, this did not happen and in his account of the sinking he dismisses this recurring claim. According to Brogden, if this had happened, the subsequent explosion would have destroyed the boiler room and engine-room platform immediately below the single funnel. As he was standing on the engine-room platform at the time the ship was hit, he was perhaps best placed of all to discount the numerous witness accounts which claimed that they had seen the bomb go down the funnel. He thought it more likely that this bomb actually fell very close to the funnel and entered No. 4 hold immediately behind the bridge. It seems likely that the Ju 88 bomber from KG30 was at least hoping to disable the ship by destroying the bridge, as had been done with the *Oronsay* earlier that day. The other bombs landed in the crowded No. 2 and No. 3 holds, and a fourth in the water on the port side. This last bomb caused severe underwater damage, rupturing the *Lancastria's* almost full fuel tanks – water could be seen flooding into a hole torn in the side of the vessel as black fuel oil oozed into the sea, creating a deadly menace to anyone who jumped into the sea.

Many of those who had boarded early were trapped or already killed deep within the ship. Within a few minutes of the attack, the ship began to list sharply to port and was quickly down by the head. Hundreds of troops jumped overboard from her decks. Due to the scarcity of lifejackets, most had to go without, and many of these succumbed quickly to the cold water and clogging oil, which entered their noses, throats, eyes and ears, as well as making it almost impossible to lift them out of the water. Very few of the lifeboats were launched due to the angle of sinking, and those who jumped wearing lifejackets risked having their necks broken by the jacket. Once in the water the survivors attempted to swim away from the sinking ship while enemy aircraft circled, machine-gunning them.

The ship sank within twenty minutes, which indicates both the severity of the damage and the probability that her bulkhead doors were not closed (due to the overcrowding). This did not allow much time for rescue, although many ships were in the area. Hundreds of men were seen clinging to or sitting on the keel as she disappeared beneath the waves. Many were singing songs as the ship foundered. Captain Sharp may have been impressed by the courage of the men in the water, but Henry Harding, another survivor, was haunted for years by the sound of the men clinging to the wreck. He described seeing thousands of men clinging desperately to the hull of the ship:

I remember there were thousands of voices singing 'Roll out the Barrel' and 'There'll always be an England', and for years afterwards I could not stand the sound of those two songs. I was turned around in the water and the next that I saw, nothing. Thousands had gone to a watery grave and I will always remember it, I can't ever forget it.

Two destroyers nearby, HMS *Havelock* and HMS *Highlander*, raced to the scene and began taking survivors aboard, as did many merchant ships present, including the *Glenaffaric*, *Oronsay*, *Fabian*, the trawler *Cambridgeshire* and the *John Holt*. As described, many of the survivors were covered with the heavy, clogging, fuel oil and some were seriously wounded; as few of the lifeboats had been properly launched, there were only a limited number of survivors in them. In the end, just 2,538 were saved. Inevitably there were many examples of heroism among those lost and saved: for example, a lone Bren gunner in the superstructure, who kept firing at the bombers even as the ship went down. However, despite the horror of the *Lancastria's* rapid demise, Captain Sharp, who survived the ordeal, stated that there was no panic on board, even up to the final moment as the hull slid beneath the sea. 'The spirit of the men in the water was wonderful, they even managed to sing whilst waiting to be picked up.'

The extent of the loss of life on just one ship was so shattering that Prime Minister Churchill forbade the publishing of news of the disaster in the UK press, clamping a 'D notice' on it. He felt that the country's morale could not bear the burden of this terrible event. In his Second World War history he wrote:

> When this news came to me in the quiet Cabinet Room during the afternoon I forbade its publication, saying: 'The newspapers have got quite enough disaster for today at least.' I had intended to release the news a few days later, but events crowded upon us so black and so quickly that I forgot to lift the ban, and it was some years before the knowledge of this horror became public.

In the event, the *New York Times*, free of British controls, broke the story, and printed some of the dramatic pictures of the disaster. They had been taken by Frank Clements, a thirty-year-old volunteer aboard HMS *Highlander*, a destroyer that was being used to ferry troops from St Nazaire harbour to the anchored *Lancastria*. Navy personnel were not allowed to take cameras on board ship but, as a volunteer in the naval stores, he managed to keep his camera with him wherever he went, and his dramatic pictures have immortalized the tragedy of the last moments of this great ship. The publication of the story in America gave the opportunity to the British press and despite the 'D notice', the *Daily Mirror* reported on 26 July that 2,823 out of a total of close to 5,000 passengers had been lost. It was the biggest loss of life in any British maritime incident.

Bodies continued to float ashore for a long time after the sinking. Eventually most of those recovered were buried in the Commonwealth War Cemetery at Escoublac, La Baule, Brittany, which overlooks the anchorage and contains about 500 graves.

To experience the sinking of his ship and the huge number of fatalities was terrible enough for the experienced Captain, Rudolph Sharp, but there was an equally sad sequel. During the First World

War he had, for a time, been commander of the *Lusitania*, but was fortunate not to be on board when she was sunk by a German submarine in 1915 off the coast of Ireland. However, after surviving the sinking of the *Lancastria*, he found himself, some two years later, commanding RMS *Laconia*. This was another large Cunard liner of 19,860 tons, which had originally been converted from passenger service to Armed Merchant Cruiser, and then once again converted back to passenger service as a troopship. On 12 September 1942, while sailing off West Africa, she was torpedoed by U156, commanded by Captain Hartenstein. The *Laconia* carried almost 3,000 passengers, including civilians and guards for the 1,800 Italian POWs, who she was conveying to America. Given the location in a shark-infested sea, few of the 2,000 survivors adrift in the sea were likely to survive. Remarkably, the Captain of the U156 surfaced and, having realized the survivors were actually mostly Italians, called other German and Italian submarines to join with him in attempting to rescue as many survivors as possible. Within a few days another two German and one Italian submarine had arrived and crammed themselves full of survivors, towing full lifeboats behind them towards the African coast. Two Vichy warships from Dakar were also sent to pick up the survivors. Then an American Liberator, from its secret base on Ascension Island, arrived in the air above to observe the scene. As the submarines had Red Cross flags draped over their hulls to show they were attempting to save lives, the Liberator left. However, in one of the most extraordinary actions involving an American aircraft, it was ordered to return to attack the submarines and the four submarines were forced to push the survivors from their decks in order to escape (although two returned and resurfaced at nightfall). Obviously many of the hitherto survivors had drowned before the Vichy ships arrived the next day. In all some 1,600 people died, leaving just 1,111 survivors. Among the casualties was Captain Sharp, who according to survivors chose to lock himself in his cabin as his ship went down. He had had enough of sea disasters.

A *Lancastria* Association was founded by a survivor, Major C.V. Petit. After his death, the Association was later renewed in its current form by some of the other survivors and children of survivors. On the first Sunday after 17 June, an annual remembrance service takes place in St Katharine Cree Church, Leadenhall Street, London, where there is a small permanent memorial to those who died.

The *Teiresias*, a smaller cruise ship of just 7,405 tons was also badly damaged on the 17th by German bombers, and had to be abandoned. Now with the sudden and catastrophic disappearance of the *Lancastria*, the tempo of evacuation increased. Troops were loaded aboard ships all night and at dawn on the 18th, ten ships, with 23,000 men aboard, sailed for Plymouth. Among them was the gallant *Oronsay*. The *Oronsay*, at almost 20,000 tons was significantly larger than the *Lancastria*. She had also been badly damaged by an earlier attack by German bombers, but had been patched up by the crew and was loaded with troops, including some of the survivors from the *Lancastria*. Despite a 10-degree list to port, she limped safely back to Plymouth.

They left behind some 4,000 troops, who were picked up in another twelve ships which left at the end of the morning. Despite the fact that seven German submarines were stationed off the west coast of France during this operation, they were unable to stop the vulnerable convoys of shipping. Meanwhile, when Admiral Dunbar-Nasmith was informed that Polish troops were on their way to St Nazaire, he sent more ships to bring them away. At La Pallice, a senior naval officer found thousands of troops at the port and requisitioned some colliers to take them off. At Bordeaux, destroyers took on board staff from the British Embassy and Consulate, as well as the President of Poland and his ministers. The Polish ships *Batory* and *Sobieski*, which had made repeated trips to England, picked up a large number of Polish and other troops from Bayonne and St Jean de Luz. Up and down the coast British ships picked up thousands of troops from smaller ports until the French Government announced on 24 July that evacuations had to cease in accordance with the terms of their armistice. In fact, the Royal Navy went on organizing evacuations from French Mediterranean ports until 14 August.

Altogether the Royal Navy was able to evacuate some 191,870 troops (including some civilians). These were not just British but included significant numbers of Allied troops who were eventually to play an important role in Britain's fight against the Germans, including the 10th Polish Armoured Brigade, which had been fighting alongside the French Army. The totals were impressive:

144,171 British

18,246 French

24,353 Polish

4,938 Czech

163 Belgians

The astounding figure of 191,870 evacuated from the area south of the River Somme must be added to the 366,162 soldiers saved from the Dunkirk area. Once again the Royal Navy vindicated its reputation for courage and flexibility in saving the British Army.

Clearly the Second BEF never achieved any of the objectives which British politicians had hoped for. Certainly at this stage of the War, the British Army was not equipped or trained to overcome the German Army. This was to take another three years. But at least many tens of thousands of men had been saved to fight another day. However, it should not be forgotten that the largely successful outcome of the evacuations could so easily have been different if they had been attempted when the Germans were better organized to intercept them. The heavy cost of the naval evacuations from Norway and the events at St Valery and at St Nazaire, with the sinking of the *Lancastria* and *Teiresias*, illustrate all too vividly what the tragic end of the Second BEF could have been.

As it was, 68,000 British troops were killed, wounded or captured during the whole campaign, and over half of them were lost south of the Somme. At least 30,000 men were prisoners of war and many were forced to march from northern France to camps deep inside Germany. According to one account this march took some six weeks. The only pleasant memory was the great kindness shown by French civilians on the way, who gave food and water to the prisoners. It hardly bears thinking about to consider the problems Britain would have faced had the total losses been of the order of 300-400,000, which is the figure that the British Government would have faced if there had been no successful evacuations from Dunkirk and from western France. Not only would the most experienced troops have been lost, together with most of their senior NCOs and officers, but Britain, having lost some sixteen divisions together with all their supplies, equipment and guns, would have been left virtually defenceless. The shock to the morale of the British people would have been devastating, and the chances of withstanding German occupation virtually nil. The concealed news of the loss of just 3,000 men on the *Lancastria* (as well as the unpublicized loss of the 51st Highland Division) underlines how sensitive the Government was to the damage that such news might have caused the British people. Churchill was fortunate that the General who argued with him prevented such devastating loss of soldiers and morale.

CHAPTER 14

Creation of the New 51st Highland Division

When Major General Fortune surrendered with his Divisional Headquarters and the headquarters of 152 and 153 Brigades, some 8,000 of his soldiers were taken into captivity. It certainly seemed like a tragic end to the history of the 51st Highland Division.

The heavy casualties and the effective destruction of such a famous division caused a very deep sense of loss throughout Scotland. The unfortunate nature of the loss of the 51st Highland Division, when it was so close to being rescued from the Normandy coast, had a huge morale effect on many. Given the dire situation and surfeit of bad news facing Britain, the unfortunate news was not widely broadcast, although the loss was all too clear to many families in the sparsely populated Highlands, who were gradually informed that their loved ones had been killed or were prisoners in Germany.

The loss of a complete division was, up until this point in the war (the much greater disasters of Greece, Tobruk and Singapore were still well in the future), a disaster of monumental proportions. It indicates what might have happened if the nine divisions of the BEF had not been evacuated from Dunkirk. As it was, although some 256,000 men were rescued, some 30,000 men had been lost from the BEF and the RAF. It was clearly a political disaster for Churchill and his policy of supporting the French. It illustrated the danger which might exist if other units were left in the path of the Germans, and the British still had tens of thousands of men left in France, most of whom were far less able to defend themselves than the Highlanders.

There is nevertheless an historic symmetry about this story. Or perhaps, as in a Greek tale, there are setbacks caused by the giant forces of fate, odysseys and the eventual triumph of the hero over adversity. Maybe this is even a moral tale, because the forces of good eventually overcame the forces of evil, for we should not ignore the fact that Rommel, for all his great military accomplishments, served an evil genius. In June 1940, 51st Highland Division, despite giving its all, fighting on the borders of France and in Normandy, was overcome in the general collapse that affected all French forces, no matter how bravely they fought. It particularly fell victim to the ambition of Rommel to distinguish himself as a military leader.

It was his driving ambition which ensured that 7th Panzer Division swept up to the coast and cut off the retreat of the French IX Corps and prevented another British evacuation.

However, clearly the whole division had not been completely lost, a significant part of it having been saved in Arkforce. Practically the whole of 154 Brigade (comprising the 7th and 8th Battalions Argyll and Sutherland Highlanders as well as the 4th Black Watch) under Brigadier Stanley-Clarke had got to Le Havre. Many members of the other brigades did get away, particularly from Veules-les-Roses. Initially it was decided that the three regular battalions (1st Black Watch, 1st Gordons and 2nd Seaforths), which had suffered such heavy casualties and been forced to surrender at St Valery, should be re-raised. 4th Battalion, Queen's Own Cameron Highlanders (152 Brigade) was also reformed and later sent to the Dutch West Indies.

Fortuitously, there also existed another division, which had historically fought alongside 51st Highland Division and also acted as a reservoir of manpower for the 51st during the First World War. This was 9th (Scottish) Division, which was recruited from the same area as 51st Highland Division. In 1938, as part of the doubling of the strength of the Territorial Army, duplicate units had been formed and 51st Highland Division had formed the 9th (Scottish) Division, which was then based in the north of Scotland. Its commander, Major General Sir Alan Cunningham, was a prime mover in having the Division renamed as 51st Highland Division in 1940. Its next commander was Major General Neil Ritchie, who later went out to the staff in the Middle East and followed Cunningham as commander of Eighth Army for a while.

Ritchie's replacement as Divisional Commander in May 1941 was Major General Douglas Wimberley, a Cameron Highlander, an enthusiastic Scotsman who had an enormous influence on the training and development of his Division. Wherever he found Scots in other divisions he inveigled them to move to the 51st Highland Division, and campaigned for an active role for the Division. Although there were fears expressed that if the 51st Highland Division were lost again, or suffered heavy casualties, it would have a very big morale effect in Scotland, it was nevertheless decided in 1942 that the Division should be sent out to join Eighth Army in North Africa. In April it was relieved of its defensive duties in north-eastern Scotland and after re-equipment it left in June on the long sea odyssey around the Cape.

51st Highland Division finally arrived in the Nile Delta in early August 1942. In the meantime, in March 1941, Hitler had decided to send his most charismatic junior general to command a small German force, which was designed to reverse the dramatic successes the British Army had achieved against the Italian Army in North Africa. Rommel travelled swiftly to Italian Tripolitania in March, and quickly began to demonstrate his dynamic ability to use outnumbered and inadequate forces to threaten and unbalance a much larger enemy, just as the main British forces were being dissipated to the futile defence of Greece and Crete. Rommel never received the full backing of his masters for his considerable achievements in North Africa, as their attention was focussed on the Russian theatre. Nevertheless, his tactical successes, combined with superior Intelligence, frustrated every attempt by the British to defeat him. His rapid advances exceeded Hitler's wildest dreams and he promoted Rommel to Field Marshal in the summer of 1942.

By the time a pale and green 51st Highland Division began to disembark in Egypt in August 1942, Rommel had defeated British forces on numerous occasions, taken Tobruk and advanced to the main British defensive line of El Alamein, just 30 miles to the west of Cairo. From there he threatened the Nile Delta and even considered the possibility of eventually linking up with German forces advancing into southern Russia. At first, the Highlanders were thrown into the hasty defence of Cairo, while in the desert to the west, the new British Army Commander, Montgomery, fought his brilliant defensive battle of Alam Halfa, which drew the teeth of the German offensive capability.

By September the Scots had been fully acclimatized and were moved forward to join XXX Corps in the El Alamein position. 51st Highland Division, with its reformed battalions, was effectively an untried formation and new to the desert conditions. Nevertheless it was given a critical role in the assaulting force and was placed in the centre of the main attack between the two highly experienced Australian and New Zealand Divisions. On the night of 23 October, a huge British artillery barrage by 832 25-pounders and 753 6-pounders commenced at 2140, which stunned the surprised German and Italian defenders. Finally, at 2210, the Scots stood up and, with fixed bayonets and pipes wailing, began to advance through the deep enemy minefields, which guarded Rommel's defences. Rommel had used the interval since his abortive attack on Alam Halfa to deepen and strengthen the Axis minefields and defensive works. Accordingly, despite being taken by surprise, the defenders were able to cling on in their deeper positions and counter-attack the British. The resulting fighting was very bitter and lasted from 23 October to 4 November. Together with the 9th Australian Division and the 4th Indian Division, 51st Highland Division suffered some of the heaviest casualties of this battle, as it took part in a succession of bloody offensives which eventually broke the German and Italian defences, and which forced Rommel to begin his retreat on 4 November.

7th Battalion, Argyle and Sutherland Highlanders had fought the Germans in the Lohwald in Lorraine during May 1940. During early June 1940, it had defended Saigneville on the Somme against the Germans and then suffered the loss of over half the Battalion (twenty-three officers and some 500 other ranks) in the desperate defence of the village of Franleu between the Somme and the River Bresle. The remnants of the Battalion were ordered to withdraw on 9 June with 154 Brigade, as part of Arkforce, sent to cover the withdrawal of the 51st Highland Division to Le Havre. As a result, they were fortunate to avoid the surrender at St Valery, and were shipped first to Cherbourg, then to Southampton, which they reached on 16 June.

Finally, two years later, the Battle of El Alamein gave them the opportunity to strike back. At 2210 on 23 October 1942, the Battalion advanced with C and D Companies leading. They took their objectives, and withstood enemy shelling and dirty tricks until, much reduced in numbers, they were relieved on the evening of 30 October. Finally, at 0615 on the morning of 4 November, the 7th Battalion (under command of Lieutenant Colonel Lorne Campbell) took its full revenge. As part of the Operation Supercharge breakout offensive, under the orders of 2nd New Zealand Division, it raced forward and captured the key German position of Point 44 on the Tel el Aqqaqir feature, thereby opening up the way for the three British armoured divisions to pursue the remnants of the retreating Afrika Korps.

The 51st Highland Division played a key role in the Battle of El Alamein, but paid a heavy price for this victory. It suffered some 2,495 casualties, the second heaviest (the Australians had 2,827), but this was a very bloody battle and resulted in such a dramatic reverse to the Axis forces that, despite substantial but belated reinforcement, they were never again able to withstand the British and Allied offensives. Without any doubt, El Alamein marked the turn of the tide in German affairs. Shortly afterwards, on 8 November, the Anglo-American landings at Casablanca, Oran and Algiers displayed the growing maritime capability of the Allies. The launching of the Russian counter-attack around Stalingrad on 19 and 20 November sounded the end of German advances in the East as it proved the resilience and growing power of the Red Army.

51st Highland Division and Eighth Army continued to pursue Rommel and his North African forces until the eventual surrender of Axis forces in Tripoli in May 1943. The 51st Highland Division had travelled some 1,850 miles across the desert, fighting Axis rearguards and overcoming the Medenine and Mareth defences. They enjoyed a victory parade in Tripoli and only sent the divisional Pipes and Drums to the final victory parade in Tunis because, by then, they and Eighth Army were preparing for the next operation. Rommel had already gone home, but he was to meet the Scots again.

51st Highland Division played a further key role in the capture of Sicily by the British Eighth Army and the American Seventh Army. Part of the Division staged in Malta, but part sailed directly from Tunisia to land on the south-east corner of Sicily on 10 July. There was much hard fighting in the mountainous terrain before the Allies drove the last of the Germans and Italians across the Straits of Messina on 17 August. On that same day Rommel was given command of Army Group B, a group of divisions held in the north of Italy to protect the southern line of the Alps. 51st Highland Division was now a veteran and dependable fighting asset with amphibious landing experience, so it left Eighth Army and was moved back to Britain in preparation for the planned cross-Channel invasion in 1944. In the whole North African campaign it had suffered 5,963 casualties including eighty-seven officers and 1,071 men killed. It is an indicator of the hard combat endured by the Division during the 39-day Sicily campaign, that it suffered a further 1,436 casualties and later commemorated this struggle with a stone Celtic Cross placed near the centre of the bitter fighting in the Sferro Hills. At the same time the Division bade farewell to the popular Major General Wimberley, who was replaced by Major General Charles Bullen-Smith of the KOSBs.

51st Highland Division was not involved in the Italian campaign as Montgomery had decided that, given its assault capability and amphibious experience, he would take the Division with him to Normandy. In the meantime, Rommel's group of forces, which had been formed in northern Italy, was moved to France in November 1943. Rommel was then given the task by Hitler, in early 1944, of strengthening the 'Atlantic Wall' of German defences designed to oppose an Allied landing. With his usual vigour he did much to improve and strengthen the defences all along the French coast and sought to gain control of the armoured resources required to smother quickly any landings.

Part of the 51st Highland Division landed at Sword and Juno Beaches on 6 June 1944, the remainder over the next six days. As such they were pitched against Rommel's forces, although he was once again away from his post when the great invasion attack was launched. 51st Highland Division was then very heavily involved in the fierce fighting in Normandy, which Rommel came to assess as being a hopeless struggle for the Germans. Although he had begun to plan how to surrender his forces to the Allies, he correctly anticipated a massive attack east of Caen by British forces. He had therefore strengthened the defences against the attack (Operation Goodwood), thereby ensuring it was effectively smothered, although he never received the reward for his prescience. On 17 July 1944, just the day before the attack by some 2,000 bombers and three British armoured divisions, Charley Fox, flying a Spitfire of the RCAF, shot up a staff car, Rommel was thrown onto the road and suffered severe head injuries. The attack took place on the road to Vimoutiers just outside the village of Sainte Foy de Montgommery. Rommel was taken to a field hospital in Berney and then to Paris, where, in a semi-dazed condition, he received the news of the 20th of July attempt on Hitler's life. At the same time, 51st Highland Division was crossing Pegasus Bridge and taking its objectives east of Caen as part of Operation Goodwood.

Although Rommel was eventually driven home to Herrlingen to recover, he knew that he had been outspoken in his criticism of Hitler and that he would never be allowed to return to duty. On 14 October 1944, he was visited by Generals Burgdorf and Maisel, emissaries of Hitler, who offered him the choice between death or suffering a humiliating public trial, and the threatened imprisonment of his family and staff in a concentration camp. This was no choice for Rommel, who said goodbye to his wife and son and left with the generals. Just 500 metres down the road he took cyanide poison and died. In an example of the usual hypocrisy of the Nazi regime he was given a eulogistic state funeral in Ulm on 19 October.

In the meantime, 51st Highland Division had not thrived in I Corps and on 26 July it was given a new commander, Major General Thomas Rennie, soon afterwards being transferred to the Canadian II Corps. With the Canadians, the Highlanders were successful in breaking through Rommel's strong defence lines around Caen and then capturing Lisieux as part of the Falaise operation. After a few days rest in Lisieux, the Division was deliberately chosen to move north, crossing the Seine and liberating St Valery-en-Caux before taking Le Havre (at the same time as the Canadians went on to liberate Dieppe, scene of their own disaster in 1942). The Le Havre operation could have been another long-drawn-out bloodbath, for the Germans, under a determined commander, had spent years building the port's defences, including digging deep tank traps dominated by pill boxes. However, at the end of August 1944, an equally determined 51st Highland Division took the town in less than three days, suffering just 123 casualties and taking almost 5,000 prisoners.

Clearing the Germans so quickly from such an important port as Le Havre was a very satisfactory result. However, before commencing the Le Havre operation, 51st Highland Division had the even greater satisfaction of liberating St Valery-en-Caux and Veules-les-Roses, where it was rapturously received by the local population. Major General Rennie (who had been captured at St Valery, but later escaped) disposed the Division in much the same areas as it had occupied in June 1940, so that units could link up with locals and find graves of relatives and friends. At last the Division could come to terms with its fate, and demonstrate its indomitable spirit and the rightness of its cause. A number of civic ceremonies of welcome were arranged at the time of the liberation and eventually (on the tenth anniversary of the surrender in June 1950), a memorial of granite was dedicated on the windswept hill overlooking St Valery, thus joining the other two memorials in Europe to this great fighting division (at the Sferro Hills in Sicily and the First World War memorial at Beaumont Hamel). On the opposite hill, near the German bunkers built to defend St Valery from the Allies, is a memorial to the members of the French IX Corps who were also lost defending St Valery. In the beautifully kept military cemetery at St Valery are buried many of those who fell in 1940. The many Scottish names in this quiet backwater of Normandy underline the bitter losses experienced by the Division in 1940.

After the celebrations in St Valery and Le Havre, 51st Highland Division rejoined I Corps and the rapid advance into Belgium and

Holland. 154 Brigade was diverted to the siege of Dunkirk, but rejoined the Division for the tough fighting in the water-logged fields of Holland near Nijmegen and Arnhem during the bleak months of November and December 1944. The German Ardennes offensive resulted in 51st Highland Division being moved south and being placed under command of General Simpson's Ninth United States Army. After initially being in reserve, it was used in January 1945 to clear the area around Marche. During February the Division came back under XXX Corps and crossed into Germany for the confused and bitter fighting in the Reichswald Forest to the west of the River Rhine. At last, on 23 March 1945, 51st Highland Division and 15th Scottish Division were given the task of being the assault divisions for the Rhine crossing. Sadly, Major General Rennie was killed during the Rhine crossing on 24 March.

After the Rhine crossing, the Division began clearing the towns and villages as it advanced towards Isselburg, and led the breakout from the river. This broke the back of the German defence and the final advance into northern Germany proceeded relatively quickly with the Division eventually celebrating final victory in Bremerhaven. However, one more satisfaction remained. Just outside Bremen, 51st Highland Division came upon 15th Panzer Grenadier Division, which claimed to be the last German formation fighting on German soil, and also to be the resuscitated successor to the 15th Panzer Division, which had been in the Afrika Korps and had surrendered in Tunisia in May 1943. The 15th Panzer Grenadier Division and all the troops in the Schleswig Holstein peninsula formally surrendered to XXX Corps on 5 May 1945. The fighting from D-Day in Normandy to Bremerhaven on the North Sea had lasted barely eleven months, but, due to the spearhead role often taken by the Division, resulted in some 9,000 casualties (including over 1,700 officers and men killed).

Thus the Division, which had already experienced an extraordinary role during the Battle of France, fighting on two fronts, and surrendering to Rommel in Normandy in June 1940, was nevertheless able to play a key role in ensuring Rommel's eventual defeat both in North Africa and Europe. Its divisional history, encompassing initial defeat by overwhelming forces, and then, after many struggles, final victory, was a miniature version of the British Army's own history. 51st Highland Division earned the right, not only to extract its own individual revenge, but also to play a key role in total Allied victory when, as one of Britain's most active infantry divisions, it took part, during almost four years of campaigning and fighting, in many small engagements and thirteen major battles, as a result of which it suffered more than 15,000 casualties.

51st Highland Division remained part of the British Army of the Rhine until December 1946. As a Territorial division it was eventually disbanded and has no current existence, but its memory lives on and its historic links with Scottish life continues.

Map 7. Deployment of 51st Highland Division in North Africa, Sicily and Northern Europe.

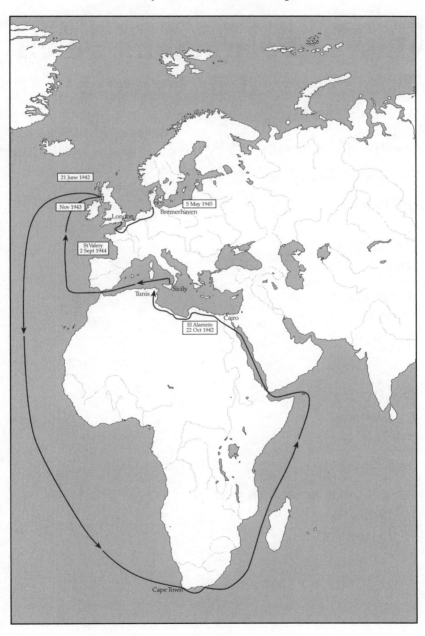

APPENDIX I

List of Formations which Served in France

FIRST BRITISH EXPEDITIONARY FORCE

BEF HEADQUARTERS

GHQ TROOPS

I CORPS

1ST DIVISION
1 GUARDS BRIGADE
2 BRIGADE
3 BRIGADE

2ND DIVISION
4 BRIGADE
5 BRIGADE
6 BRIGADE

48TH (SOUTH MIDLANDS) DIVISION
143 BRIGADE
144 BRIGADE
145 BRIGADE

II CORPS

3RD DIVISION
7 GUARDS BRIGADE
8 BRIGADE
9 BRIGADE

4TH DIVISION
10 GUARDS BRIGADE
11 BRIGADE
12 BRIGADE

5TH DIVISION (MOVED FROM III CORPS)
13 BRIGADE
17 BRIGADE

50TH (NORTHUMBRIAN) DIVISION (MOVED FROM III CORPS)
150 BRIGADE
151 BRIGADE
25 BRIGADE

III CORPS

42ND (EAST LANCASHIRE) DIVISION
125 GUARDS BRIGADE
126 BRIGADE
127 BRIGADE

44TH (HOME COUNTIES) DIVISION
131 GUARDS BRIGADE
132 BRIGADE
133 BRIGADE

Construction Divisions in Rear Areas

12th (Eastern) Division

35 Brigade

36 Brigade

37 Brigade

23rd (Northumbrian) Division

69 Brigade

70 Brigade

46th (North Midland and West Riding) Division

137 Brigade

138 Brigade

139 Brigade

Defence of Boulogne

20 Guards Brigade

Defence of Calais

30 Brigade (mostly drawn from 1st Armoured Division)

Independent Command (under French Army)

51st (Highland) Division

152 Brigade

153 Brigade

154 Brigade

1st Armoured Division

2 Armoured Brigade

3 Armoured Brigade

1 Support Group

Additional Reinforcements for the Second British Expeditionary Force

52nd (Lowland) Division – 2nd British Expeditionary Force

155 Brigade

156 Brigade

157 Brigade

1st Canadian Division – 2nd British Expeditionary Force

1 Brigade

2 Brigade

3 Brigade

Additional Units formed in the L of C

Beauman Division

A Brigade

B Brigade

C Brigade

Bibliography

Brooke, Lieutenant General Sir Alan, 'Operations of the British Expeditionary Force from the 12th June 1940 to 19th June 1940' (Report dated 22 June 1940), Supplement to the *London Gazette* dated 22 May 1946.

Bryant, Arthur, *The Turn of the Tide*, Collins, London, 1957.

Butler, J.R.M., *Grand Strategy*, vol. II, HMSO, London, 1957.

Churchill, Winston S., *The Second World War* (abridged by Denis Kelly), Cassell & Co. Ltd., 1959.

Colville, John, *Gort, Man of Valour: Field Marshal Lord Gort, VC*, Collins, London, 1972.

Dancher, Alex and Todman, Daniel, *War Diaries 1939-1945 of Field Marshal Lord Alanbrooke* (edited by Len Deighton), Weidenfeld & Nicolson, London, 2001.

Deighton, Len, *Blitzkrieg*, Jonathan Cape Ltd., London, 1979.

Edgar, Donald, *The Day of Reckoning*, John Clare Books, London, 1983.

Ellis, Major L.F., CVO CBE DSO MC, *The War in France and Flanders 1939-1940*, HMSO, London, 1953.

Fraser, David, *Alanbrooke*, Collins, London, 1982.

Gilbert, Martin, *Winston S. Churchill: Finest Hour 1939-1941*, Heinemann, London, 1983.

Guderian, General Heinz, *Panzer Leader*, Michael Joseph Ltd., London, 1952.

Höhne, Heinz, *The Order of the Death's Head*, Pan Books, London, 1981.

Jackson, Robert, *Dunkirk*, Cassell Military Paperbacks, 1976.

Karslake, Basil, 1940: *The Last Act*, Leo Cooper, London, 1979.

Liddell Hart, Basil, *History of the Second World War*, Cassell & Co., London, 1970.

Linklater, Eric, *Calais*, Pan Books Ltd., London, 1981.

Mellenthin, Major General F.W. von, *Panzer Battles 1939-1945*, Cassell & Co., London, 1955.

Moore, William, *The Durham Light Infantry*, Leo Cooper, London, 1975.

Powell, Geoffrey and Powell, John, *History of the Green Howards*, Leo Cooper, London, 1992.

Remy, Maurice Philip, *Mythos Rommel*, Ulstein Heyne List Verlag GmBH & Co., Munich, 2002.

Rommel, Field Marshal Erwin, 'History of the 7th Panzer Division, 19 May-25 September 1940', *The Rommel Papers* (edited by Basil Liddell Hart), Collins, London 1953 (in the IWM Library).

Shirer, William L., *The Rise and Fall of the Third Reich*, Secker and Warburg, 1961.

Spears, Major General Sir Edward, *Assignment to Catastrophe*, vol. II, 'The Fall of France, June 1940, Heinemann, London, 1954.

Thompson, Major Paul W., *Modern Battle*, Penguin, London, 1941.

Warner, Philip, *The Battle of France, 1940*, Cassell Military Paperbacks, London, 1990.

Index

161

Canadian Army:
  II Canadian Corps, 148
  1st Canadian Div, 45, 84, 87,
    105, 108-10, 115, 117-20,
    123, 125-6
Canal Line, 26, 28-9, 33-4, 47-8,
  55, 102
Cérons, 98
Chamberlain, Neville Prime
  Minister, 6
Charbonneau, Gen, 129
Cherbourg, 2, 30, 69, 88, 90, 99,
  103, 110, 123, 126, 145
Churchill, Brig, 151 Bde, 57
Churchill, Winston, Prime
  Minister, 1-3, 5, 46, 55, 65, 69,
  77, 83-9, 103-4, 108, 111-23,
  136, 140-1
Clements, Frank, 136
Cojeul, River, 56, 58
Commandos, 88
Cunningham, Maj Gen Sir Alan,
  142
Curtis, Maj Gen, 33-4, 57
Czechoslovakia, 6

D
Daily Mirror, 136
Dakar, 137
Darlan, Adm, 87
Deighton, Len, *Blitzkrieg,* 83
Dender, River, 54-5
De Margerie, 83

De Gaulle, Gen Charles, 71, 83-
  4, 86, 93, 95-6, 104, 112
De Vuillemin, Gen, 83
Dieppe, 35, 95, 148
Dietrich, Sepp, 43
Dill, Gen Sir John, 83, 85, 104-
  6, 112, 114, 116, 118-19, 125
Dinant, 14-15, 127
Douai, 36, 48
Doullens, 26, 29, 30-1, 39, 59-60
Dunbar-Nasmith, Adm Sir
  Martin, 131, 138
Dunkirk, 2, 16-19, 21, 24, 27-8,
  36-7, 43, 46-9, 51, 54, 61, 63,
  85, 88, 90, 101-5, 113, 139,
  141, 149
Durdent, River, 96-7
Dutch Army, 9
Dyle, River, 8, 19, 54, 101, 105

E
Ecurie, 59-60
Eden, Anthony, 83, 106
Egypt, 108, 144
El Alamein, 3, 21, 108-9, 143-6
Elkins, Comd RN, 97
Ellis, Maj L.F., *Official History,*
  21, 118
Escaut, River, 19, 54-5
Eu, 81, 94
Evans, Maj Gen Roger, 70

Ironside, Gen, 19, 21, 23, 55, 104, 107

Ismay, Gen, 83

Italy, 3, 13, 84, 146

Italian Tripolitania, 143

J

James, Adm Sir William, 97, 125

John Holt, 135

K

Karslake, Lt Gen Sir Henry, 89, 107-9

Karlsruhe, 12

Kennedy, Brig, 117

Kennedy, United States Ambassador, 119

Kirkup, Brig, 26, 59

Kitchener, FM Lord, 54

Kleist, Gen Ewald von, 13, 15, 53, 61-2

Kluge, Gen von, 12

Königsberg, 12

L

Laconia, HMT, 137

Lancastria, HMT, 2, 113, 125, 129, 131-40

Lanquetot, Gen, 45

Leeb, Gen Wilhelm von, 9

Le Havre, 3, 23, 75, 87, 89, 94, 96-7, 99, 112, 125, 142, 146-7

Le Paradis, 43

Lille, 14, 16, 127

Lisieux, 3, 148

Loire Valley, 83, 110, 132

Lusitania, 137

Lutz, Gen, 68

Lutzow, 12

Luxembourg, 7, 12, 66

M

Maginot Line, 7-8, 10, 21, 29, 66, 69, 76-8, 80

Manstein, Gen, 15

Marine Bde, 45

Marne, First Battle of the, 45

Marne, River, 6

Maroeuill, 59-60

Marshall-Cornwall, Lt Gen, 114, 123, 126

Marseilles, 84, 88

Martel, Maj Gen, 56-9

Metz, 76

Meuse, River, 8-9, 14-15, 41, 47, 63, 80

Mohnke, Wilhelm, 44

Montgomery, Lt Gen Bernard, 21, 106-9, 115, 144, 146

N

Nanteuil, 128, 131

Narvik, 12, 85, 90

New York Times, 136

New Zealand Army:
    2nd New Zealand
        Division, 144-5

Nicholson, Brig, 46, 69

Normandy, 2-3, 14, 21-3,
    25, 32, 80, 85, 88, 98,
    109, 125, 141, 146-9

Normanforce, 123, 126

North Africa, 3, 83, 87, 144,
    145, 149

Norway, 2, 11, 90, 129, 131-
    2, 139

O

O'Connor, Gen Sir Richard,
    53

Operation Aerial, 129-40

Operation Cycle, 97, 123-7

Operation Dynamo, 17, 49

Operation Goodwood, 147

Operation Supercharge, 145

P

Paris, 32, 53, 83, 85, 104,
    131, 147

Paris Conference, 31 May
    1940, 65, 104, 111

Péronne, 24, 29, 70

Pétain, Marshal Henri, 83,
    86-7, 131

Petit, Maj C.V., 137

Petre, Maj Gen, 25-6, 28

Petreforce, 28

Plan 'D', 8

Polforce, 34

Poland, 5-6,

Polish Army:
    10th Polish Armoured
        Bde, 139

Pownall, Lt Gen Sir Henry,
    55, 109

Pratt, Brig, 58

R

Rambures, 31-2

Rennes, 23, 89, 110

Rennie, Maj Gen Thomas,
    147-49

Reynaud, Paul, French
    Prime Minister, 83-4, 86,
    104, 116, 118, 131

Rommel, Maj Gen Erwin,
    2-3, 13-14, 40, 51, 61, 89,
    96, 125-7, 142-9

Roosevelt, Franklyn D.,
    United States President,
    119

Roupell VC, Brig George,
    30

Royal Air Force, 7, 21, 84,
    91, 103-4, 108, 112-13,
    133, 141:
    Air Component, 7